SPIRITUAL

M000031075

HOW TO BECOME A

GREAT SPIRITUAL

LEADER

TEN STEPS AND A HUNDRED

SUGGESTIONS

Leonard Doohan

ISBN: 978-0-9910067-6-2

ISBN: 099 1006-763

THE AUTHOR

Dr. Leonard Doohan is Professor Emeritus at Gonzaga University where he was a professor of religious studies for 27 years and Dean of the Graduate School for 13 years. He has written 24 books and many articles and has given over 350 workshops throughout the US, Canada, Europe, Australia, New Zealand, and the Far East. Leonard's recent books include *Spiritual Leadership: the Quest for Integrity*, published by Paulist Press in 2007, *Enjoying Retirement: Living Life to the Fullest*, published by Paulist Press in 2010, *Courageous Hope: The Call of Leadership*, published by Paulist Press in 2011, and The *One Thing Necessary: The Transforming Power of Christian Love*, published by ACTA Publications in 2012.

HOW TO BECOME A GREAT SPIRITUAL LEADER
TEN STEPS AND A HUNDRED SUGGESTIONS

Table of contents

STEP ONE: Rediscover great leadership.   **1**
1. Think about leaders and leadership in a new way.
2. Desire to become a great leader.
3. Confront the failures of leadership.
4. Appreciate the challenge to greatness.
5. Focus on who you are as a leader.
6. Integrate leadership and spirituality.
7. Let your style of leadership give the world something to think about.
8. Take courage in your pursuit of spiritual leadership.
9. Become part of a new generation of leaders.
10. Emphasize the Christian dimensions of your leadership.

STEP TWO: Emphasize remote preparation   **15**
1. Strive for self-control.
2. Look beyond the wasteland of contemporary leadership.
3. Long to be different.
4. Change your focus from self to others.
5. Make time for leisure, reflection, and prayer.
6. Train yourself to see and look at things in a different way.
7. Study leadership.
8. Rejoice in other people and their successes.
9. Be joyful, optimistic, and enthusiastic.
10. Appreciate that this world's values are not enough.

STEP THREE: Set a new direction for your leadership

31

1. Understand the meaning of conversion
2. Realize that change is necessary for transformation.
3. Be willing to let others guide you.
4. Accept pain and loss.
5. Identify stages in conversion.
6. Appreciate when everything just comes together.
7. Choose a good crisis.
8. Set a new direction.
9. Pursue ongoing conversion both personal and organizational.
10. Examine your life constantly.

STEP FOUR: Accept your vocation of leadership   **47**
1. Accept leadership as a vocation.
2. Journey inward to identify your destiny.
3. Maintain a sense of humility.
4. Do no harm as a leader.
5. Realize you are called to be nothing less than a leader.
6. Nourish the call of leadership.
7. Recognize you are called to love.
8. Be the best you can be.
9. Maintain the dream.
10. Value gift, acceptance, and receptivity.

STEP FIVE: Implement your call in a vision   **63**
1. Recognize the pre-requisites of vision.
2. Identify the components of a vision.
3. Repair the past.
4. Be a servant-spiritual leader.
5. Develop the skills for visioning.
6. Be a leader of hope.
7. Foster habits of mind and heart.
8. Appreciate there is no vision without community.
9. Develop the building blocks of leadership.
10. Make all decisions based on your vision.

STEP SIX: Live your vision with courage and perseverance **81**
1. Institutionalize the vision.
2. Awaken others to a new vision.
3. Keep a hold on the vision.
4. Embody the vision in a spirituality.
5. Remember your prophetical calling.
6. Emphasize the transcendent.
7. Focus on your charisms and the community's charisms.
8. Remember your role as healer.
9. Pay the price of maintaining the vision.
10. Celebrate the vision.

STEP SEVEN: Establish supports for your spiritual leadership **97**
1. Develop strategies against excessive stress.
2. Align your leadership with your values.
3. Create space for yourself.
4. Find a supportive community.
5. Seek enlightenment from a strong personal faith.
6. Become a contemplative leader.
7. Accept the power that is offered you.
8. Be aware of stages in your growth as a leader.
9. Develop enthusiasm for the leader's journey.
10. Clarify the image of God who constantly draws you to leadership.

STEP EIGHT: Evaluate your leadership: an artist's challenge **113**
1. Focus always on the common good.
2. Start from authentic wisdom.
3. Remember the foundations of leadership.
4. Enthrone justice.
5. Work for concord.
6. Seek peace.
7. Embody the appropriate virtues.
8. Check the effects of good leadership.
9. Avoid all forms of tyranny.
10. Watch for the signs of bad leadership.

STEP NINE: Work with your followers-disciples.   129
1. Spread the message.
2. Channel others' gifts.
3. Support co-workers and followers.
4. Find ways to teach the people who work with you.
5. Make sure co-workers know how important they are.
6. Build a trusting environment.
7. Oversee co-workers' development.
8. Confront with compassion.
9. Lead followers to personal transformation.
10. Give followers freedom and let them go.

STEP TEN: Accept ten personal reflections   145
1. Affirm people.
2. Build good social interactions.
3. Always do more than you ask of anyone else.
4. Reflect and pray.
5. Live simply as a leader.
6. Choose to work with opposition.
7. Be a free voice.
8. Plan from hope.
9. Keep working life in perspective.
10. Create new projects.

STEP ONE

REDISCOVER GREAT LEADERSHIP: AN INTRODUCTION

1. Think about leaders and leadership in a new way.

I would like to offer this book as a challenge to the reader to think about leadership and leaders in a new way. This current book presents the challenge, why not become a great spiritual leader, and attempts to answer the question, how do you become a great leader? Several books deal with the "what" and the "how" of leadership, whereas this one focuses exclusively on "who" is the leader and who he or she can become personally and spiritually. So, I am writing this book to indicate the need for integration between leadership and spirituality. Here, I have less interest in what leadership is and does—in fact my previous books dealt with those issues—and more interest in who has the potential to be a great leader and how he or she can attain it. Thus, I have chosen here to leave aside the discipline of leadership and focus on the inner transformed life that helps one become a great leader. This book is a logical development from my previous two books on leadership. *Spiritual Leadership: The Quest for Integrity* presented the foundations for spiritual leadership. *Courageous Hope: The Call of Leadership* focused on some new key concepts that must permeate all modern leadership.

Nowadays, we use the word "leadership" too loosely. We use it for many business people who are the antithesis of leadership, who have no desire to lead people anywhere, and in fact prey on others rather than guide them. We use it for many religious administrators who have contributed next to nothing to the spiritual development and renewal of their people. We use it for many healthcare executives, pledged to heal, who withhold their money from those most in need of healing. Titles such as executives, CEOs, presidents, bishops, generals, commanders, trustees, senators, all seem to suggest leadership, but recent history and experience confirm that there is no such automatic connection. Many are good people but are not prepared to be leaders in today's complicated world.

I want to share with you the importance of authentic spirituality for leaders. We all know what leaders need to do, the skills and behaviors they need, and their ongoing refocusing as a result of experiences. From my many contacts with people struggling to be good leaders, I am convinced that who the leader is and the life direction he or she chooses are determinative of success more than anything else. Response to destiny is critical for quality leaders. That is why in this book I will focus on the person of the leader and the steps he or she must take in order to facilitate the transformation necessary to be a contemporary spiritual and effective leader. My hope is that readers will participate in this process of transformation. This book is to help you on the pathway towards your quest to be a great leader. However, the first step is to think about leaders and leadership in a new way.

2. Desire to become a great leader.

I want to help those of good will who want to become great leaders. We seem at times to be in an irreversible stall when it comes to leadership development. Many people are given authority and power way beyond their competence, and followers must often protect themselves from the irredeemable incompetence of their bosses. We have to acknowledge, with great sadness, that we are surrounded with failures in leadership. However, there are many men and women of good will who could become great leaders to the benefit of society, but at times they just do not make it.

Sometimes they cannot bring themselves to make the first demanding steps that could lead to quality leadership, possibly they feel unworthy, or sometimes they have initial fear of the demands that lie ahead. Although endowed with lots of good will, some have been misguided, trained with wrong priorities, led to believe they do not have what it takes to become a great leader, or have been encouraged to model themselves on other leaders who lack the genuine focus of authentic leadership. Clearly, we do not want more of what we have had to tolerate. Some programs and courses on leadership are a hindrance to the kind of leadership that is needed today; thus, some become very competent in skills that harm rather than help organizations and their members. It is sad to see many continue in their immature approaches to leadership because they do not know how to break away from the inappropriate methods and training that have been suggested in the past, or because they lack the guidance they need, or because they lack the strength of will to accept the sacrifices that contemporary leadership implies. Some even resist the call they hear in the depths of their hearts to serve others in a transformed leadership.

I am not undertaking this particular project because I think I see things no one else does. We have benefitted so much from the insights on leadership presented by many scholars and practitioners. I have detailed references to the great contemporary experts in leadership in my previous two books on leadership. However, I have worked all over the world with wonderful people, many great leaders from all walks of life, and have learned so much from them, both in appreciating what led to their successes and in identifying the unfulfilled yearnings of others. At the same time I have seen so many men and women who long to give themselves to the service of others, but just cannot get things moving. They work tirelessly, read and study all the latest insights into leadership development, and attend conferences and workshops that they believe will help. There comes a moment when one needs to pause and ask "Is what I am doing helping me become a great leader?" Often the answer is no; neither the system, nor the leadership model, nor the means suggested are working. Then it is time to stop and acknowledge that we must move in a different direction if we want to foster great leadership, and I offer the reflections in this book to challenge you to do that. If you are a person of good will and long to serve others by your leadership, there is every chance you can become a great leader, provided you focus on the appropriate preparation and consciously participate in the stages of growth indicated in the chapters ahead. This is a menu of floating ideas that can enrich your commitment.

3. Confront the failures of leadership.

I would like to contribute to removing the great question-mark that hangs over leadership. Great institutions, whether in politics, business, social life, healthcare, or religion, are shadows of what they could be. It is heartbreaking to see contemporary "leaders" floundering around in their lack of competence, integrity, and ethics, often struggling for short term gain at other people's cost, loss, and pain. Others are hung up on ideological points, often non-essentials, while losing sight of the original vision of their organization. Still others arrogantly think they know what is best for their followers, when everyone knows that managers are responsible for most of the mistakes in any organization. Many of our "leaders" are failures, and we spend more time and energy trying to get rid of bad leaders than we do trying to cultivate good ones. As a result, nowadays, so many followers simply ignore their so-called leaders or work hard to manage their leaders' defects. Let us face it, most of the people we call leaders are at best good managers with a sprinkling of inspiration now and again. Rather than being served by leaders, we often identify our leaders as oppressive forces who put shackles on the powerless. In the middle ages the citizens were allowed one day a year when they made fun of their leaders; it was called "The Feast of Fools." Nowadays, it would be a daily event, as our organizations are laid waste by fools who claim to lead us.

Not all problems are the result of incompetence, nor of greed and addictions. When you consider leaders in politics, business, and even religion, you may not know what they will do with their leadership once they attain it, but even before they start you know what they will be unable to do. Leaders today work within limitations imposed by lack of education and training, ideologies, psychological problems and agendas of followers, ideas of their backers and benefactors who cannot be offended, and strictures imposed by higher ups. Unhealthy organizations and systems have limiting effects on the good will of men and women who strive to be leaders, reminding us of the need of organizational conversion and of the need to prophetically denounce the arthritic institutions in which they operate.

I seek leaders who will get us beyond the cloud that overshadows today's leaders and move us to a new reality in which men and women, gifted with management and leadership skills, have something more to offer. They will be dedicated to a vision of hope within the plan of God, will have all the needed skills, attitudes, and behaviors of leadership, will be willing, even eager, to serve followers and the common good, and will have the fortitude needed to endure the pain of being called to serve. We need a new kind of leader, a spiritual leader, motivated by a profound spiritual experience that has touched him or her and is now willing to live in light of this experience. This book gives the steps one can follow to do this, and I hope you will be willing to move in this new direction and answer the call to serve others.

4. Appreciate the challenge to greatness.

I propose a renewed appreciation for the personal challenge to greatness. The last couple of decades have given us a lot of insights into leadership: knowledge, skills, and attitudes. However, much of this has clouded the reality that leadership is a vocation. You can have all the skills in the world, but they will not make you into a great leader if you lack the inner spiritual transformation that produces a vision of hope within the plan of God. Moreover, the conviction that everyone is called to participate in leadership has been a great motivator within organizations. However, while everyone is called to participate in leadership not everyone is called to be a great leader. If everyone is a leader, then of course, no one is, and the call to great leadership loses its attraction and fades away. The notion of distributed leadership has blocked the appreciation of the need of exceptional, great leaders. I appreciate that most change percolates up from the grassroots and does not filter down from high up in a structure. Nevertheless, only a great leader perceives this, acts upon it, and guides the process.

We cannot get out of the mess we are in without leaders who appreciate their call to greatness. Like prophets of old, they will be criticized, lonely in their vocation, viewed as outsiders, and rejected for being different. However, all forms of social institutions today are in crisis. No one looks to the majority of today's "leaders" with hope, since most of these people depress us. Even organizations that claim to know about the future hopes of humankind are more frequently attached to the past and need to be dragged screaming into change that can lead society to renewal.

I hope some readers of this book will be willing to prepare themselves to be leaders. Call is something we cannot control, but those willing can prepare themselves so that when call comes they will be ready. Of course, no one prepares himself or herself to be great, but rather to respond to the need to serve others. Greatness is never pursued for itself; it is always a byproduct of service. There is something noble and satisfying about giving oneself to the betterment of others, to the pursuit of goals that enrich humankind. This is a calling that leads to greatness; leadership is the medium through which one expresses one's deepest values.

When we look at the responses of people throughout the world to their current leaders, and when we see just how much people are longing for men and women who will lead them out of the mess we are in, then we see that there is a deep yearning for new leaders who will give themselves to public service. We need leaders who will focus on others and not on themselves, on selfless service and not on accumulation of power or wealth, on what is best for each one and not on promoting the latest trivia of their agendas. This book offers a way forward for those willing to take it and gives suggestions as to how one can nurture the call to leadership.

5. Focus on who you are as a leader.

We generally presume that leadership is what you do, I am interested in who you are. Leadership makes things happen and works to achieve common goals. There are multiple approaches and no singular formula for success. There are many incarnations of leadership, and we can learn so much from them. However, many who have the skills of leadership have turned out to be total failures as leaders. Even now there are so many "leaders" who are burdens to society, and there are not many honorable resignations from the failed leaders of contemporary organizations. Their addiction to greed in money, power, position, prestige, condemns followers to a limbo, and such people are blocks the emergence of true leaders.

Leadership is not determined by what you do but by who you are. What you then do is a result of the inner values that have transformed your life. Authentic leadership touches every aspect of one's personality. What a leader does results from the fact that he or she is a reflective and contemplative person, hears a call and responds to it, lives with integrity, works for a shared vision, and makes choices based on spiritual values. The leadership journey is a way of transmitting one's deepest and most cherished values. Such a leader is competent, motivates followers to values such as justice, service, community, and love. We can all gain so much from contemporary insights into leadership; they are great but inadequate. Today's leader must go deep within himself or herself to find the authentic self, a purpose in life, and personal destiny, for leadership is who you are and not just what you do.

This book is written for men and women to wish to integrate their leadership with the values they hold dear in the depths of their hearts. It is an invitation to think about oneself and the kind of leader one wishes to become. For such people leadership is a way of living one's humanity; it is not an add-on, or something one does for a while, in a job; it is the one and only way a man or woman lives. By always living inspired by values of vision and hope he or she will impact those around. Thus, one gives oneself to the service of others as the only way to be authentically present to this world. Leadership is a response to a call felt deep within one's inner spirit and it requires that a person embody this call in a personal vision of life.

6. Integrate leadership and spirituality.

I propose there are no great leaders without a commitment to spirituality. If size, balance sheets, status, personnel numbers, salary, profits, power, and so on, determined great leaders then some Wall Street executives, healthcare industry CEOs, politicians, even religious administrators would be great leaders, and obviously many are not. The problem with many of these people is that they make enormous sacrifices of their integrity to remain in power. Rather, inner values, convictions, spirit, and openness to transcendence are the qualities that determine great leadership. We must give serious consideration to the intangibles of spiritual leadership, if we are going to change the kind of approach to leadership from what we see now to what we must attain.

Spirituality refers to a person's efforts to become the best he or she is capable of being, to become his or her authentic self. Spirituality is the ordering of our lives so that everything we do reflects the values we hold deep within our hearts—honesty, justice, integrity, service, community, hope, and love. In some ways, spirituality is all about relationships; our relationship with ourselves—always striving to be the best we can be; our relationships with others—treating them with respect, seeking what is good for them, serving them, pursuing the common good; relationships with community organizations and structures—utilizing them for the betterment of people and not as ends in themselves; and relationships with God before whom we must judge ourselves and the kind of leadership we espouse.

So, in this book I seek the integration of human knowledge and leadership development with an integral spiritual calling, for spirituality is part of who we are, and we can never be our true selves without it. Leadership without spirituality would be a body without soul. Spirituality gives life to our leadership. A great leader must point to values beyond this world and work within the framework of leadership in light of convictions regarding values beyond the immediate horizon of life. Thus, spiritual leaders climb the heights of leadership by living and sharing values of the Spirit, by leading with spiritual conviction, by being constantly motivated by the vision of the future in hope. I say all this because I believe in a vision of life within the plan of God. All this contrasts with the betrayal of values we have witnessed in so many failed leaders of recent decades.

7. Let your style of leadership give the world something to think about.

I offer an approach to leadership that will give the world something to think about. I just cannot take failed leadership anymore! I am fed up and disgusted with our "leaders" in all walks of life; angry at the disastrous situations in politics, at the disgusting aspects of business greed, at the pathetic loss of direction from religion. I know leadership development is always within constraints, but we have to stop this roller coaster, initiate a shake-up of leadership that for too long has been immersed in incompetence, corruption, and secrecy, and has done so much harm to all organizations including religion. We must insist that people in charge be leaders; but this might be too much to expect given the culture of arrogance, corruption, greed, and selfishness that we see all around us and the desperate need of pseudo leaders to preserve the status quo. The steady and relentless erosion of values, of service to the common good, of generous dedication, of a vocational response to God's call, must be replaced by a renewed dedication to spiritual leadership and to these values. This will happen slowly at first, one step and one leader at a time, but it will be contagious, and eventually will reach a critical mass, and then lots of people will think of leadership in a different way.

Our contemporary world evidences both the "kingdom of darkness" and the "kingdom of light," but the former seems much more powerful than the latter. Good leadership is rare. Current forms of leadership are not working; even small problems become intractable, and we lack people who can break through the barriers that prevent resolution of important issues in politics, social life, and religion. Key people in the world need to think about new visions, priorities, relationships, goals, means, and strategies. We must find leaders who can create interruptions in the way we have been thinking, force us to stop and reflect, and open us to something different. We need leaders who will not prolong the best of the present, but lead us to the future from a vision of hope. We need leaders who will not embody the worst of humanity, but lead with an awareness that there exist two horizons to life—this one and the one beyond. We need leaders who will not pursue their own selfish goals, but lead from love, justice, and mutual appreciation. We need leaders who will not be fixated with getting to the top, but lead through an extensive commitment to service of others.

There is always tension in leadership between the here and now and the there and then, between the already and the not yet. We need leaders with a new understanding of commitment, who work out of simplicity, who seek direction in contemplation, and who can unlock the potentials of the heart; leaders who act deliberately, always making decisions in light of what is the most loving thing to do. Their action is enlightened, they humbly revise all they do, and they are always involved in ongoing self-formation. The "kingdom of darkness" will not like this approach, but it is needed, and it is the focus of this book. Leaders today need always to review what constitutes good leadership and bad leadership.

8. Take courage in your pursuit of spiritual leadership.

I want to encourage the fainthearted in their pursuit of spiritual leadership. I am convinced that the road to leadership greatness passes through spiritual renewal. I urge each of you readers to become the leader you are called to be. Only a small percentage will be interested because of the addictions to power, status, and money that attract and hinder so many in their pursuit of leadership greatness. But there are others, and I would like to tap the potential of these leaders to be great. What we need to acknowledge from the outset is great leaders always pass through the challenging experience of conversion. My hope is to help you develop a process that leads to personal transformation and thus enables you to become a great leader. Great leaders are not born, they gradually grow and mature into who they are capable of being for the benefit of others. Ordinary people can become great leaders; we must let the best rise to the top of leadership.

Leadership is a work of the heart, a courageous heart. In this book's approach, a leader is motivated by a vision of hope. Since leadership is a vocation, the leader is not struggling to move forward, but he or she is being drawn forward by something or someone greater than himself of herself. So, even the fainthearted can take courage and move with confidence, for leadership is not what you do but what God is doing in and through you. The best leaders are not always the most knowledgeable or talented, but those who are open-hearted, open-minded, and receptive to the call and challenge of God; those who let themselves be guided and directed for the good of others. These leaders can influence others as far as is needed, can motivate others to leadership, are happy to disappear from the scene and give credit to others, and can then reappear in a new venture to lead in a new way.

So often today, leaders are unknown and unsung heroes, simple people with big hearts. They begin their work locally and gradually have an impact on large sections of society. Many are fainthearted and prefer the hidden life. Sometimes they stay there and effect local change, sometimes they are recognized and brought into public view and appreciation. Even television channels celebrate these gifts to community service. So to each of you, reading this book, even if at times you feel lost, I say you can become a better leader, you can become the leader you long to be. May this book challenge you to evaluate all aspects of your leadership and courageously move in the direction of growth and maturity.

9. Become part of a new generation of leaders.

I wish to contribute to preparing a new generation of leaders. We must give more to the next generation of leaders than the last one and the present one have given to us. We have lost respect for leaders, and organizations we had looked to for insight and formation in leadership have largely failed us. Business schools, management programs, even religions have contributed very little to leadership in recent decades; in fact, they are partly to blame for the mess we are in. They have offered very little in their teachings and insights, and they have given us few models or examples to emulate. Most of these training or formation programs are known for the mediocre leaders they produce.

We can only be successful in preparing a new generation of leaders if we can change the current way of training them. This means the curriculum of business and management schools needs to change. The focus of nursing education and the preparation of all medical personnel, including physicians, needs to focus more on service, integral healing, patient-centered care, and availability. Seminaries and ministry training programs will need to develop totally different leadership training programs to prepare those who wish to minister in religion. Enough is enough! What we have been using has not worked, and we need something different. Above all, we need a change of mentality from an emphasis on training to one on transformation.

This book offers an action plan for people of good will who would like to be leaders for the coming generation. Those who are willing to give themselves to the service of others in leadership must first of all prepare themselves, and we will together look at the specifics of this preparation. Men and women of good will must set a new direction for leadership and this is attained through a conversion that leads to transformation. Part of this new direction is the awareness that leadership is a personal vocation, and we must identify the basic components of this call and how to nurture it. Leaders must then implement this call in a vision of leadership that is quite specific and demanding. This vision will need to be institutionalized and thus lived out with courage and perseverance. Those who wish to be great leaders must establish supports that can protect, nourish, and grow their leadership in service of others. Wise leaders will constantly evaluate their leadership, determining what is good and what is bad, what must continue and what needs to be changed. The final step in this action plan is when leaders can pass on their vision and values to their followers so that a new generation can participate in the shared vision. These are the chapters of this book.

10. Emphasize the Christian dimensions of your leadership.

I want to emphasize the specifically Christian contribution to leadership. Jesus Christ is a model of what leadership can be. His action of washing the disciples' feet epitomized his approach to servant leadership. He described himself as a good shepherd who was always willing to lay down his life for his followers. He insisted that all his followers must, like him, be ready to serve others and never seek to be served by others. Jesus' life and ministry offer us the major components of a model of leadership that is still valid today. Jesus' leadership was based on a spiritual experience and before each period in Jesus' ministry we find him immersed in a close relationship with God, a specific experience that prepared for the period ahead. Jesus led by calling people together in loving solidarity; he never focused just on those with whom he worked, but influenced everyone with whom he came in contact. The vision Jesus pursued implied change at all levels of society, in fact he offered a new comprehensive way of looking at life, as he sought not only personal transformation but societal transformation too. One of the characteristics of Jesus' leadership was that he rarely dealt with the powerful people of his day— except to denounce their corruption, rather he empowered others, especially the fainthearted, poor, and uneducated. He gave no priority to status, power, wealth, or privilege, but gave voice to everyone. He broke stereotypes, rejected social boundaries, and accepted diversity. In fact, his leadership went well beyond religious renewal to include a comprehensive reform of political, economic, and social systems.

In a Christian vision of leadership, people are first, not products or processes. This means trust, vision, hope, and spirit are a leader's primary qualities. It requires that leaders need energy, enthusiasm, creativity, combined with humility if they are to serve the common good. These leaders will be trusted and trusting, inspired and inspiring, transformed and transforming, healed and healing, influenced by a vision and influencing others to be visionaries, and motivated by hope while bringing hope to others.

In a Christian vision of leadership the intangibles of leadership are more important than the tangibles. The former are constitutive components of leadership, the latter are means, techniques, skills, and strategies. Leadership training has generally focused on the latter, seeing those components as the real, hard issues of leadership development. This has been an incorrect emphasis and has led us down the wrong path. The intangibles, often considered the vague, soft issues of leadership, are very important. They create a new environment, a new sense of purpose, a new spirit of community, a new commitment to shared vision and values, and all these components are important in contemporary leadership. They are not secondary but integral to leadership success and moreover they significantly affect the bottom line in any company.

Insights of the Christian tradition will permeate the chapters of this book, as we immerse ourselves in developmental stages in spiritual leadership. I hope each reader will find this approach enlightening, challenging, and irresistible in his or her vocation to leadership. When all is said and done, leaders are disciples, followers of the Servant Leader.

STEP TWO

EMPHASIZE REMOTE PREPARATION

S piritual leadership is the result of a personal call to serve the common good, a vocation from God to lead others to shared values within the framework of organizations, social interactions, and community development. The call is a gift and no one earns it. However, this call is never given to people who are unprepared. Thus, the one commitment men and women of good will can make is to prepare themselves for leadership, so that if and when the call comes they will be ready. If you wish to become a spiritual leader, you must first of all undertake a serious preparation that establishes the qualities you will need for what lies ahead. In this chapter I offer ten components of this preparation. Other components can help, but these ten are essential; they are qualities that you can develop now, that you will later need in your efforts to become a great leader.

1. Strive for self-control.

In the last couple of decades, we have witnessed a lot of reckless, wanton uncontrolled greed—whether for money, power, ideological purity, and so on—from many managers who have destroyed financial institutions, healthcare organizations, service industries, religious priorities, and even nations. Some have even pleaded for government regulations or international interventions because they recognize that they cannot regulate themselves. They know they are out of control. As a leader you need to live ethically, with integrity, and this means first of all being able to control your own negative tendencies. This first step implies breaking away from self-centeredness through a regime similar to an exercise program; this self-control is a form of spiritual conditioning for one's mind, spirit, and heart. Mature leaders generally know their own weaknesses, are aware of their own sinfulness, are sadly conscious of the basic evil in our world, and they know they need to develop self-control.

Self-control is really a re-education of one's values, focusing on one's central goodness and moving away from self-centeredness to other-centeredness. This requires reflection, charity towards others, identification of potential addictions, and moderation of one's passions. All this requires a spirit of sacrifice, a commitment to avoid exaggerations, a monitoring of one's time, and a willingness to reject comparisons with others for the satisfaction of one's own presumed betterness. Spiritual leadership does not just happen. It demands a specific preparation that prudent people take to guarantee they will never become like the sick or inadequate leaders we have seen in recent years.

If you wish to become a spiritual leader you must limit negative concepts, attitudes, and behaviors in yourself. This gradual removal of the negative components of one's life is a preparation to become a leader who serves others without ever evidencing these failures. These preliminary efforts include self-control in the use of food, drink, drugs, sex, or an exaggerated emphasis on one's own comfort. It will also include the elimination of an acquisitive tendency, a possessive accumulation of things whether one needs them or not. This emphasis on possessiveness in money, goods, and services leads to a false exaggerated notion of one's own importance. If you do not remove all these forms of self-gratification and self-centeredness, then your leadership is destined to failure.

As you aspire to great leadership you will also need to assess your attitudes to others. When you see in yourself a desire for power over others, then you must root this out immediately. Many tendencies we notice in ourselves are perhaps only small at first, but they are never stationary or static; they are always growing. Those "leaders" who disturb us today were not always the way they turned out; they just allowed small negative attitudes to grow, unchecked. If you put down others, expect others to serve you, use others for your benefit, or worse still abuse others—you must counteract these negative tendencies by systematically doing the opposite—not power over others but service, not abuse of others but daily signs of respect, not manipulation of others but mutuality, not exaggerated competitiveness but collaboration, not using others but celebrating their gifts.

Great leadership requires the priority of people over organizations. Those who work within organizations cannot make decisions exclusively on money matters, or thoughtlessly terminate people and bring suffering to their families just to give balance to the fourth quarter earnings. People who want to be spiritual leaders stem the negative and at times abusive elements in a working environment. In times of preparation men and women with potential for leadership reassess their attitudes to organizational life and institutional development, so that they foster just approaches to people within organizations. If you yearn to embody spiritual leadership you must appreciate organizational defects and pledge to remove them from your own life. Self-control practiced in preparation for leadership helps us become our best selves, to develop just relationships to others, to establish a sense of mutuality, community, and shared vision and values.

2. Look beyond the wasteland of contemporary leadership.

Every generation presents us with outstanding leaders, and our own is no exception. However, we have also faced overwhelming failures of leadership, so much so that leadership today is a dark place where at times we are afraid to go. So much harm has been done by our leaders' cold hands of malice, selfishness, arrogance, and greed that we are filled with anger and even more with anguish at what has happened. Any analysis of political, business, or religious leadership easily leads us to despair. We often feel immersed in a numbness and helplessness as we wonder where all the good leaders have gone.

Men and women who are willing to offer themselves to the service of leadership must mourn the failures of contemporary leadership, savor that failure, face, identify, express disgust at the greed, loss of values, selfishness, and incompetence we see in abundance. All this is part of a process of purification of the destructive models of leadership. But creating the alternative seems too much for us to achieve; it is a dark night in which we are helpless without the transformative interventions of God. Acknowledging our helplessness in face of overwhelming negativity is also a valuable experience of preparation.

Christianity has traditionally identified seven serious failings that go against everything that Christianity stands for, and we generally refer to these failings as the seven deadly sins, or the seven capital sins. They are a summary of the wasteland of failed leadership that men and women of good will must strive to overcome if they wish to be great leaders. These seven deadly sins are pride, avarice, lust, anger, gluttony, envy, and sloth. It is appropriate to apply these failings to an analysis of one's own life but, more importantly, to interpret them in relation to social and specifically leadership failures that we must prepare ourselves to avoid.

When you dedicate yourself to become a spiritual leader, you are at the same time purifying life, and this not only makes you a better leader but a better spouse, parent, friend, and a member of the human community. Such a person rejects the deadliest sins that corrupt one's life. Pride is the sin of those who arrogantly show disrespect for others' needs and rights to justice, who always expect to be given special treatment, who do not like to be challenged, who expect a big payoff when terminated for incompetence, who feel only they are responsible for success. Avarice is the sin of those who are never content with what they have but who always want more of everything that makes their own lives materially better. They deprive others of what they need simply to have more themselves. Lust is the sin of those who use their place in an organization for sexual satisfaction, or who lust for power, position, status, and benefits. They create luxurious offices and lust for ever bigger clumsier firms, too big to fail. Anger is the sin that appears when some people are challenged, asked to change, asked to do what is just, asked to bring balance into their organizations. Such people get angry at others' negative evaluations and reviews, and turn their anger against subordinates who do not achieve unrealistic goals. Gluttony is the commonest sin among many in leadership today as they want more and more salaries that are out of control, golden parachutes for achieving very little. They are gluttonous for respect, status, fringe benefits, the adulation of others, and offices and personal treatment beyond reality. Today's greedy always want more, never want to share even a little of what they have. They are also greedy to have everything their own way. Envy is the sin of those who become sad and angry at others' successes, at others who get contracts they wanted, at others' payment packages that they think they deserve. Sloth is the sin of those who do nothing about perennial problems, make no effort to resolve situations that cause suffering to millions, take easy solutions, or do nothing to protect workers' dignity. While always active for their own benefit, they are lazy in taking care of others. Spiritual leaders who see these failings in others must have the courage to say to them "get away from me; I don't want to be like you."

3. Long to be different.

Sooner or later, a man or woman who gives himself or herself to leadership through service sets a new direction for life, one that is different from what we have seen in the failed or inadequate leaders we know. This is a first step in the transformation of leadership and you must want it. To succeed as a leader you need a totally different way of thinking about leadership and about yourself as a leader. You must long to be different. Leadership becomes your way of revealing your own form of exploration.

A great leader is set apart for the service of others. This does not mean that a specific person is any better than others, and one should always avoid unhealthy comparisons. However, if you wish to prepare yourself for leadership, you must long to be different than other people who do not feel this yearning. As a leader in the making you have a vision of yourself in relation to community. This is part of a process of discovering your deepest personal needs, hopes, and dreams. It means moving away from failure and mediocrity, and striving to be the best you can be; a longing emerges to be a different kind of leader than we have so frequently had.

This longing to be different demands focusing on others and not yourself, on others' achievements and not on your own, on service and not climbing the promotional ladder, on others' gifts and not your own, on others' competence and not your authority, on taking care of others and not self-aggrandizement, on seeking the best for others and not what is in it for you. In leadership all this leads to a different set of priorities: not self but others, not power but service, not authority but collaboration, not control but facilitation, not personal vision but shared vision, not telling others but listening to them.

Changing your attitudes and behaviors is a long process, but it begins quietly in your heart, when you feel moved to choose a different direction in your way of leading. This will not just happen by chance but will require self-scrutiny and ongoing discernment. Strangely enough, this process is not one of acquiring new ideas, skills, or practices, but more one of getting to the heart of your leadership. It is more a project of sandblasting rather than adding another coat of paint! peeling away false values and letting the best of oneself shine through. Longing to be different comes to mean longing to be your true self. In the center of each one's heart there is a zone of natural goodness, and that is where you find the values of authentic leadership. Clearly, you need skills of implementation and management, but leadership is always a matter of heart, spirit, and soul.

A person like you who wants to be a spiritual leader needs to make this longing practical in daily decisions that show how you seek and are determined to be different. If you prepare well, then what is ordinary to some people will never be ordinary to you. The only thing each one can do is live one's own truth. But this needs lots of careful and deliberate preparation.

4. Change your focus from self to others.

Many men and women in positions of potential leadership are too self-centered. They do not care about other people except as means to attain their own goals. However, successful leadership requires an ability to capitalize on other people's contributions to an organization. Preparing for leadership must include self-training to emphasize the movement away from self-embeddedness to self-transcendence with the goal of stressing the central importance of others. Spiritual leaders appreciate that while achieving the goals of the organization, it is also their task to respond to other people's deepest needs, hopes, and dreams. They focus not on their own goals but community goals because they believe in people. At first this will result from deliberate effort but gradually, with constant practice, it will become a natural reaction. Preparation consists in training oneself to respond more appropriately. After all, the leadership problems of recent years have arisen because men and women who could have been leaders instead gave constant priority to themselves rather than other people.

Changing focus from self to others begins with simple everyday practices, deliberately appreciating some positive quality of someone else, and taking no one for granted. This includes listening carefully to others when they speak and listening also to their non-verbal communications. It means giving credit to others whenever possible, showing appreciation and gratitude for something they do, recognizing their personal gifts and achievements. This preparation must foster respect for others, a sense of mutuality, and even reverence for other people. It means giving people visibility and prominence. At the same time you will discover yourself in self-gift.

A spiritual leader will show others how important they are to the organization by healing any potential problems in the working environment, by clarifying and refocusing roles so that there is no misunderstanding, by setting goals together so that everyone feels a part, by examining channels of communication so that everyone is kept informed, and by establishing means of recognition.

Furthermore, focusing on others means valuing others, delegating authority to them, encouraging them to participate in decision-making, getting out of their way when they accept responsibility, and celebrating their successes. So, this preparation means removing any injustices that afflict others and then cherishing others and their gifts, even drawing out others' gifts and nurturing their creativity. This part of preparation means learning how to make a difference to other people's lives and committing oneself to live and work for community growth. Clearly, these attitudes and behaviors are ongoing throughout your life as a spiritual leader, but men and women who yearn to become exceptional leaders must begin in small ways by deliberately changing the focus from self to others. In fact, once you are in an important leadership position, it is almost too late to learn these simple interpersonal skills and you are left to live off the efforts and preparations of former years.

5. Make time for leisure, reflection, and prayer.

Leadership needs reflection and even contemplation, so that as a leader you can keep things in perspective, be inspired by people and the world around, appreciate and savor both the good and the bad that happens, and be open to a sense of wonder, awe, and mystery. Preparation for leading requires a balance between the need for lots of energy and inner peace. Often our world is too noisy for spiritual leadership, too cluttered to touch the extraordinary in serious reflection, and too immersed in trivia to engage in discussion on meaningful issues of life. Those who yearn to be outstanding leaders become restless until they can find the inner peace that comes with leisure, reflection, and prayer. As a leader you must learn to discover the divine action and intervention in every event of life and you can only do this when you prepare to be nourished, strengthened, and enriched by the fullness of the present moment. You must learn to create silence within yourself.

An inspired leader prepares himself or herself to be a great spiritual leader by self-training in leisure, reflection, and initial prayer. Such people become more perceptive and profoundly aware of their role in the world. They develop an attitude of openness and receptivity to the deeper levels of events around them; even an openness to the grace-filled actions of God within them. They become at home in their own situations in life and find that the environment around them is a true guru—a teacher, guide, and healer. In the quiet time they create, they learn the values of community and become aware of how much they can learn from others. Leisure, reflection, and initial prayer help develop quality attentive presence in a leader, and this fosters appreciation of self, others, and the world. In fact, the preparation for reflective leisure enables a leader to learn how to integrate values in a holistic viewpoint and at the same time to be open to new priorities.

So, part of the preparation for leadership is to train yourself to become a person of leisure, reflection, and prayer. You do this by taking time to rest, read, relax, and even recreate. In this restfulness you can rethink things, rejoice in life, refocus your commitment, renew your energy and values, and even rejuvenate yourself. You will also need to be aware of negative attitudes and behaviors common in modern society—compulsiveness for work, constant complaining, attitudes of negativity. Leaders in the making must avoid these situations as well as avoiding those people who embody these negative non-reflective approaches to life.

In addition to the above preparations, a leader should learn how to set aside time each day for at least initial forms of prayer. Prayer starts with relaxation and silence and moves on to concentration and awareness of the present moment. It requires that one let go of cares and worries, accept oneself as one is, generating a sense of forgiveness and reconciliation with oneself and with others. There follows a phase of focusing contemplatively on life and on God, expressing hopes and intercessions for self and others, and ends in gratitude. These simple preparations for prayer will develop later into mature prayer but for now these preparatory stages are enough.

6. Train yourself to see and to look at things in a different way.

One of the important qualities of a spiritual leader is to see things that no one else does. It often means such a leader can analyze situations and see connections that no one else does, or maybe set out a vision that responds to people's needs even when the people did not establish the vision themselves. Often a spiritual leader sees into workers' reactions, good or bad, and perceives why they react in a given way. Such a leader identifies goodness or potential negativity where others do not. Then again, a spiritual leader appreciates common elements imbedded in disparate data.

This ability to see things no one else does comes from years of preparation, when he or she who aspires to be a good leader deliberately looked at things in a different way.

When you look at something—a difficult situation, a relationship, a community problem, and so on—and look at it carefully and intensely, you glimpse aspects of a situation not appreciated at first glance. Looking skillfully at any situation or decision that needs to be made, you learn to assess potential negative side effects to the good and potentialities for good in the negative. If you give adequate time to analyzing an issue—a decision, a project, a mission statement, and so on—you can discern the best possible outcome, but this process takes time and skill. In a world where many leaders try to force us to their point of view, a spiritual leader learns to appreciate how everyone's point of view can contribute to a shared vision. In a world characterized by the blame-game, a spiritual leader constantly strives to distinguish between an issue to be criticized and a good person involved in it. This is part of the wisdom of a spiritual leader. He or she strives to look at the big picture, all sides of an issue, making effort to relate it to a future of hope. When this is done, seeing and looking at things in a different way is a preparation for visioning.

As a person who is interested in preparing to see and look at things differently you can engage in a series of practices that facilitate this acquired skill. You will need four preliminary qualities—stillness, inspiration, concentration, and silent appreciation. Spiritual perception does not emerge out of a cluttered life. So a leader needs to know how to be still with a decision or problem, be inspired by its potential for good, concentrate on available options, and silently appreciate the potential transformation that can result.

Part of seeing what no one else sees is to listen like no one else listens, so practice listening intently to any conversation, to a piece of music, to the sounds of nature. Then try to look at something in a way you never have before, paying attention to some ordinary scene or event or interaction of people until you see something you have never seen before. A further aid to seeing and looking differently is simply to sit still, do nothing, and totally relax, looking at and savoring every aspect of an experience. Then the leader to be needs to concentrate on a situation carefully, affirming what is good and equally carefully seeing the negative in need of transformation. With calmness, aided by breathing exercises, a leader prepares for spiritual perception that brings a special dimension of wisdom to all he or she strives to do. Finally, as a spiritual leader you need to look at the whole context of leadership and see the guiding hand of God, working through the people, events, and the mission of a shared vision.

7. Study leadership.

Anyone who aspires to be a great leader should never presume that he or she has achieved that goal. Like physicians, leaders can be general practitioners, inner leaders, or specialists, and like physicians they must study, learn the needed skills, and keep up to date with developments in their discipline. Spiritual leaders must be good at the normal and exceptional management skills. There is little value in having a spiritual vision if the person has no ability to implement it. In recent years, we have seen tremendous developments and enrichment in leadership studies, and they have given us four approaches to learning about leadership. Some scholars and practitioners focus on information, research, and quantitative analyses, and thus they enrich our knowledge base. Others stress the learning available through interactions in workshops, and this facilitates new skills. A third approach provides experiences that show what leadership can be like, and this challenges our attitudes and behaviors. The fourth approach encourages people to make the inward journey to discover self-identity, and this makes us more aware of our responsibility, vocation, and destiny as leaders. Anyone seeking to be a good leader benefits from all of these. If you want to be a skilled leader, you must learn; read, attend conferences and workshops, be active on the web, participate in discussions, learn from each other's strengths and weaknesses, gain insight and perspective from a mentor, and review and evaluate whatever one does. Nowadays, there are many valuable journals, newsletters from leadership centers around the country, and annual conferences that can keep one up to date.

However, while all this is essential, you must ask how this study affects you. Some who think of themselves as leaders always know the latest insights from books or articles and can recite with ease the latest comments of leadership gurus. However, often they rarely change the essential values of their leadership, even though they may well implement the latest practice for a while. What one does as a result of this information is important. Does it all help to change attitudes, behaviors, and sense of call? Does it contribute to transformation? The important issue in utilizing constant study as a preparation for leadership is the ability to utilize it within the framework of a developing vision of leadership. Later, as one grows as a leader, ongoing education will always be necessary, but then whatever is judged to be valuable will be integrated within one's existing vocational approach to leadership. In times of preparation one must critically evaluate the input from study and discern its usefulness in attaining the goal of spiritual leadership. Eventually the insights of study must go beyond information, attitudinal change, and behavior modification to a profound synthesis with who you are called to be. Study is not a sideline issue but it becomes an enriching part of who you are, your destiny as a leader. Now and again you read something and when you have finished you are different. May your reading be conducive to transformation.

8. Rejoice in other people and their successes.

Organizational goals are best achieved by communities in which each member feels valued. Workers perform better when they are trusted, admired, and feel good about themselves. As a person who wants to be a spiritual leader you must learn how to work with other people so that they feel appreciated. Leaders need to be aware that they attain their goals with and through others; that they are incomplete without the gifts of others. This means giving time to others, getting to know them, and being truly present to them. A leader can show followers that he or she cherishes their presence and talents by giving them opportunities to utilize their gifts, delegating responsible work to them, collaborating, sharing mission values, practicing subsidiarity, and empowering them.

It is also part of preparation for leadership to become skillful at celebrating people's successes, honoring their achievements both informally and formally. A leader should always know what workers have done that merits a word or gesture of recognition. It might be just stopping someone in the corridor to share a compliment and to let them know you appreciate what he or she has done. It could be a more formal gathering—although never perfunctory—to celebrate successes. In each case it is a way of giving others visibility. Celebrations are a way of conveying gratitude, affirmation, shared joy, and further anticipated successes. Celebrations also reinforce the organization's values, serve as motivation for others to strive for success, and nurture people's gifts. Learning to rejoice in other people and their gifts is an important preparation for leadership. Of course, it is a wonderful part of family life and daily friendship too.

When a person learns how to rejoice in other people and their successes, there follows a series of positive consequences both for the leader and for followers too. First, by appreciating the gifts of others one is also preparing oneself for a sense of humility, when one discovers how important other people are. Second, this brings a new perspective to one's leadership, realizing all are important in a common enterprise. Third, celebrating others' contributions generates confidence and therefore hope of more involvement in the future. Fourth, this work of preparation produces a sense of common ownership of the mission of the organization. Fifth, in preparing oneself to constantly appreciate the gifts of others a leader is also building up a sense of community. Sixth, if a leader dedicates himself or herself to genuinely create this environment of mutual appreciation then indirectly he or she will control the negativity that frequently inflicts a community of workers.

Perhaps the most important effect of preparing oneself to appreciate others and their common efforts for the good of the community is that a leader begins to sense the value of love as a major component of leadership. Celebrating others' successes is a way of encouraging the heart of others and cultivating initial aspects of the role of love in leadership.

9. Be joyful, optimistic, and enthusiastic.

Joy, optimism, and enthusiasm are three interconnected concepts in the life of a spiritual leader. He or she needs to be vibrant, cheerful, full of interests, and excited about life. All leadership has its times of oppression, justified reactions of anger, and feelings of resentment. A leader has to put up with a lot of negativity and personal criticisms while trying to keep optimistic and to maintain positive motivation of others. In times of preparation, when problems may be minor, a person who longs to be a good leader must begin to develop positive attitudes to work, a resistance to any negative, and a hope-filled context for the long haul. In this preparation these three components, joy, optimism, and enthusiasm, play critical roles.

Joy is an essential component of the life of a spiritual leader, preceding and concluding every stage in leadership. Optimism is the attitude of a leader who takes a hopeful view of things, expects positive outcomes, and looks forward to achieving good developments through leadership. Enthusiasm describes a leader who is guided by the values of God (en theos = in God) and can approach his or her work with confidence. These three qualities enable a leader to live with courageous patience, resilience, innovative thinking, openness to the future, and encouraging hope. Such leaders know difficulties are an integral part of leadership, they can bear the pain and frustration being a leader brings, and they can manage the discouragement, depression, and rejection working with others produces.

If you wish to be a leader of joy, optimism, and enthusiasm you must cultivate these values in times of preparation. Avoid the company of pessimists, of those who always grumble, criticize, and wallow in negativity. Do not react immediately to anything negative that happens, but pause, reflect, remind yourself of the big picture, and gain some distance. Savor the negative, seeing the harm that it does to yourself, to others, to the community, and to the shared mission. Remember this pain and suffering so as to learn from it and focus your spiritual vision on faith in daily resurrections that reflect your convictions about life.

Look for the good in all that happens, and remind yourself of how often positive developments result from events that started out negatively. Focus your heart on your mission and recommit yourself to it and to all the struggles that are integral to its achievement. In the presence of others, try to control non-verbal reactions, negative movements of your body and face that communicate your displeasure. Instead, remember to portray understanding, if necessary without approval, for something unfortunate that happens, and when necessary criticize constructively. Think about how much you like doing what you do. When appropriate smile, be affirming, remind everyone to be optimistic. This kind of preparation can test the strength of one's faith in the goals of leadership. Most groups contain about fifteen percent who can always find something negative to criticize in any situation. Spiritual leaders must maintain joy, optimism, and enthusiasm no matter how people react. Since this is so hard, one must prepare remotely to maintain these qualities.

10. Appreciate that this world's values are not enough.

Men and women who aspire to be great spiritual leaders learn to appreciate the real world in which they exercise their leadership. It is a world with two horizons of life and interaction; the immediate world of human discourse and a horizon of life beyond this one that gives meaning to our daily lives. Training to be a spiritual leader and steadily working through the various preparatory steps we have reviewed in this chapter help a leader catch glimpses of a realm of reality beyond this one. In striving for self-control and looking beyond the failures of leadership we see how this world is often a counter pull to the world beyond. We become ashamed of this world's values and seek something beyond us that can purify the negative trends of this world. Longing to be different and striving to transcend ourselves shows us how we yearn for something beyond ourselves. Reflection, contemplation, and efforts to look at life differently are all components of a preparation to give increasing value to the horizon of life that gives meaning to this one. However, our preparation for leadership cannot direct us to isolation and artificiality; rather, we must study components of leadership in the present world, learn how to treat people with respect and affirmation, and gain perspective on what it means to live out our leadership enthusiastically in the presence of God.

Leaders need to prepare themselves to appreciate the limitations of our ordinary world that sometimes appears as the kingdom of darkness, and to look beyond to the kingdom of light. Leaders must prepare themselves to make decisions in view of the real and practical needs of this world, while making decisions in view of the values of the world beyond this one. No one makes a selfish decision when he or she makes it in light of death and transition to life beyond this one. In fact, this is the only real question for human beings—what will happen at the end of life. Then we approach the present in light of the future. This preparation focuses on seeing links between the two horizons of life. One makes decisions in the "here and now" in light of the "there and then."

Part of our preparation consists of deliberately looking at connections. When you see something you consider unjust, ask what you think justice would be and why. When you see something you consider abusive, abnormal, why do you view it this way? Ask yourself what you consider your purpose in life and where you think this judgment comes from. Then again, when you find you are loved unconditionally, for no reason, how do you explain this? What do you value most in life—maybe justice, equality, love, community, goodness—why do you think these are important values? Each of these daily occurrences stimulates reflection and suggests that explanations must include a value system beyond this world's.

A further part of this self-training is when a potential leader to be not only asks how to make certain decisions, but why. It implies looking at things that surprise one—good or bad—and ask why they produce that reaction. It certainly includes thinking about why you are loved and loveable and realizing everyone else is too. It means asking yourself for answers to puzzling attitudes you meet in other leaders you know and finding that this world's values are an inadequate explanation.

STEP THREE

SET A NEW DIRECTION FOR YOUR LEADERSHIP

Anyone who wishes to become a spiritual leader needs to appreciate the importance of the transforming experience of conversion. This is the transition from former ways of leadership to new ways of leadership. It is crucial that a leader understands what is happening and what needs to happen to facilitate this change and to allow it to happen. It is a major change in life, a painful experience, and a learning experience. A person who crosses this threshold will see himself or herself differently, will appreciate others differently, and will identify the impact on life of transcendent values. One's conversion is the beginning of a new chapter in leadership.

1. Understand the meaning of conversion.

The word "conversion" literally means "a change of heart," and it was part of the first public statements of both John the Baptist and Jesus Christ, and thus became a key value in Christianity's vision of life. In Jesus' time the heart was thought to be the source of both emotions and knowledge, and conversion came to mean accepting a completely new outlook on life. Jesus said it was necessary if one wanted to live the way of life to which God calls us, to live in the reign of God. Conversion is never over and done with, but here we look at a first decisive step to change direction and to get a new outlook on life that includes new values. For those who strive to be spiritual leaders there is a profound experience similar to a second conversion that is a movement away from the debilitating false values of leadership and a movement towards the priority of values of heart, spirit, and soul in dealing with others.

Conversion is a change of direction, an effort-filled determination to become the self one can be and to become the kind of member of community to which one feels called. This is a moral and value-filled decision. Conversion is an erosion of formerly appreciated values. It demands authentic humility, a knowledge of one's own limits and frailty, and the acceptance of others with their hopes and dreams. It is a shocking experience of clarity, an awful awareness that one's life has to be different. It gives rise to a radically different set of values, such as a preferential option for service, a prioritizing of values of the heart, a realization that one is here to do the Lord's work, and an overwhelming sense of the need of prayer. Conversion always leads a person to focus on ultimate values.

Above all, conversion is a personality altering experience, an existential choice, a crisis. It implies a peaceful acceptance of self, an awareness of one's own human limitations, an abandoning of the masks we wear, and a determination to be a different kind of leader than one has been. Conversion means walking away from false approaches to leadership that clutter the soul and distract from insight into the realities of spiritual leadership. Conversion consists in a new image of oneself, one based on one's authentic strengths; it challenges one to develop these new strengths for the benefit of all around us in organizations we lead and in communities we serve.

Conversion is a spiritual awakening that first challenges us to address our counterfeit selves then to ascend to values of the Spirit. It raises the level of conduct, of ethical aspirations, and of visioning, and it triggers deep determination to embody these in actions. Conversion calls each one to live on a new plane of being and action, allowing oneself to be influenced by God and by values of a horizon of life beyond this one. Conversion is the beginning of a process of transformation, the initial acceptance of a call to a new way of life. It is a pivotal point in one's leadership adventure.

The preparations we saw in the last chapter help ready a person for conversion. It is not clear whether conversion begins with a movement of the heart or an intellectual conviction, both are necessary and are intimately related. Once a person recognizes the challenge to conversional change, he or she must nurture this with reflection and prayer, so that it becomes embodied in a vital conviction that impacts life. Then the leader needs to make this vital conviction real in daily decisions. Thus, conversion challenges the leader to rearticulate the values of heart and mind in the normal activities of leadership.

2. Realize change is necessary for transformation.

Conversion is essentially a change in the direction of one's life within the context of faith—from bad to good, from good to better, from better to the best one can be. It is an experience that is both active and passive; a person works hard to change the direction of his or her leadership but at the same time accompanying events, including the descent of grace, move a person to become different. It is all about change—change of outlook, change of attitudes, change of values. Change is good, often necessary, sometimes we need to change direction in order to preserve the values we hold dear. Leaders need to be ready to change before they are forced to.

Change that leads to transformation often starts when a person finds that he or she constantly feels empty and dissatisfied no matter what he or she does. A person may experience distractions that are the result of pulls and counterpulls in life, leaving one with a sense of aimlessness. Then again one may long to leave behind the comfort of old ways and old structures, sensing they no longer serve any purpose. At times one becomes oppressed with the leadership failures all around and wants to be different.

Change is a fact of life, but even change has changed, as it is now rapid, profound, and always present. We live immersed in it and need to discern which change can lead us to transformative conversion. When faced with change we must ask the right kinds of questions, analyze the change, critique its relevance, recognize its learning potential, and see where our commitment is needed.

Then we must have the courage and perseverance to let go of old values and make a deliberate choice for a new horizon.

The desire to change is not just because of negative pressures such as the ones mentioned, but change and conversion are results of the call of God, the gifts of the Spirit. That is why the preparations we discussed in the last chapter are so important, since they make a person more receptive and ready him or her for the descent of the Spirit and the grace-filled call of God.

So, as you aspire to be a great leader you must welcome change and especially those crucial major changes we call crises. The original meaning of crisis is judgment or discernment; it is a turning point that requires a new kind of outlook on life. This is when great leadership comes to the forth; on other occasions we are left with only management. In other words leadership is the ability to handle crises creatively, caringly, and productively. It is intimately linked to conversion for individuals and organizations.

Leaders realize the importance of change; not simply organizational or product adaptation, but personal and organizational change that brings about new approaches that depend on morally different values. Change is important in leadership development when it contributes to setting a new direction in vision, mission, and values.

3. Be willing to let others guide you.

Arrogant self-sufficiency blocks many who could be leaders from access to the extraordinary all around them, in themselves, in others, in communities. In conversion a person responds to a call from outside oneself and finds he or she is being drawn to a better approach to life. It is not something a person earns, but rather a gift. Above all, conversion is what God is doing in us, but often others contribute too. This becomes a learning experience that we are at times, often in critical times, guided by God and by others and not by ourselves. Our contribution is to place no obstacles in the way of transformation, to be open and receptive, and to humbly realize our own emptiness and need.

In setting a new direction in your leadership you will find you are not moving forward, improving, achieving new goals, but rather you discover you are called, gifted from outside, drawn, and missioned. You find you are enriched by loving, listening, and learning. This is no bogus empowerment such as some pseudo-leaders utilize, but an internal movement of Spirit that leads us to self-transcendence. When we witness the bankruptcy of so many leadership styles and systems, we find truth still lives in the dialogical interaction between ourselves, God, and others.

A leader is always separate from followers but at the same time intimately connected with them. You guide and challenge followers but also learn from them, can be inspired by them, and find your greater self with them. A spiritual leader who is convinced of this profound interrelationship and interdependence will make sure to create an environment of open communication, mutual trust, unity, and group purpose. Such a leader will also evidence humility towards his or her own views, strive to focus on others—individually and in teams, have the courage to say what needs to be said, challenge others to achieve their best, and always maintain some personal distance from task and people for ongoing renewal. In this way he or she creates an environment in which a leader can learn from others whose guidance can at times be deliberate and at times readily accepted even though the givers remain unaware of their impact.

A leader can sense and receive the guidance of others even when they evidence reticence to share their views. Then the leader shows his or her own honest vulnerability, lives with inner integrity and gives example of commitment. Moreover, the leader coaches and guides others' participation by influencing others to be visionaries, and fostering self-leadership in followers. These approaches inspire commitment to a shared vision. Above all, such a leader constantly shows love and encouragement, taking care of followers, criticizing constructively, bearing the pain, and generating enthusiasm. These qualities pay high dividends in the participation of followers.

When a leader reflects on how much he or she learns from others and internalizes this conviction, then this becomes part of conversion's new outlook on life. The leader appreciates that one is not autonomous but interdependent with followers and can learn much from them whether they intend to teach or not. A good spiritual leader can hear followers' voices of concern or interest, and can weigh these carefully learning from their non-verbal communications. In other words a leader can be inspired by what lies unconscious in the vision and hopes of followers. All good leaders need to be willing to let others guide them in these varied ways.

4. Accept pain and loss.

Setting a new direction in your life and leadership is stressful. As a leader, you abandon a past you thought was fine and now launch out to an unknown future, and there is always pain. A leader experiences at the same time hope in a new choice and regret for former ways of leading. The conversional experience of setting a new direction brings insecurity, darkness, and a threat of lost good things. However, every worthwhile step in leadership development has its price to pay, and you must die to certain forms of superficial leadership if you are to move to spiritual leadership.

A leader who passes through a conversional experience moves from a set of old values to a set of new ones and feels that the ground beneath him or her is giving way. Having seen that there is more to leadership than one first thought, the leader stops seeing things in one way and starts seeing them in a new way. This experience at first shocks the leader, leaving him or her discouraged at having spent perhaps a long time dedicated to the wrong values. The leader-to-be savors the pain of this loss, for he or she must become convinced in the depths of soul that former values are inadequate. As the leader struggles to set a new direction in life, he or she accepts the pain and loss, knowing that only when one is truly emptied of false values can one be filled with new and transforming ones.

Accepting the pain associated with one's conversion helps one to help others in their pain. Leadership includes this dimension of healing offered to others who experience pain. There are three components of a leader's approach to the pain that arises in organizations. First, one should remember the pain, his or her own and others', especially the dangerous life-changing memories of pain. Second, a leader should commit to solidarity with those who for one reason or another are in pain. Third, it is helpful for a leader to listen to the stories of others' pain, so that the leader can avoid situations that could cause stress and suffering to others.

Memory of pain, solidarity in pain, and listening to the stories of those who suffer are three tasks that leaders can practice as people of faith to help them improve their spiritual leadership. Such leaders, caught up in others' pain can draw on their inner strength, endurance, hope, and love, as they long to bring healing to others and to organizations. Their hearts go out to others who suffer, they feel a profound sadness for those who cause it, and they admire those who live peacefully through the trials that working in organizations can bring. They can sense how good the absence of suffering can be and determine to remove it from the lives of others.

Responding to the pain of others means a new view of the world and of what it means to be human. When suffering is inflicted deliberately or results as a consequence of a leader's self-centered choices it is always contrary to humanity. Responding means a conversion—a change of heart, a new outlook on life. Leaders must think about the causes of suffering and whether they are the cause of suffering for anyone else. They should reflect on whether there is anything in their lives and work that causes suffering to others. Accepting pain is an integral part of setting a new direction in life.

5. Identify stages in conversion.

There often comes a time in a leader's life when he or she acknowledges that "I feel sad to be what this situation calls me to be." "I know I am not true to myself." "My heart does not yearn for this, and when I attain it I still feel empty." "What I am doing doesn't work, doesn't feel right, and even seems unjust." We often see contrasting styles in leadership that attempt to address these insufficiencies. Many "leaders" are lazy, irresponsible, half-hearted in their work, and find their lives are mediocre when they yearned for so much more. Others are workaholics, substituting quantity for a balanced life of values and quality involvement. Some of these men and women want to change the direction of their lives. Dissatisfaction can be a good first step in the transformation that conversion brings.

I suggest a simple approach to conversion that considers three stages in its development. This is modeled on the typical conversion experience identified in so many people and groups in recent times. As mentioned previously, a person who passes through a conversion actively contributes to the changes and also finds that due to others or to situations around him or her some things happen that are passively accepted. This active-passive dynamic produces the desired change.

The first stage of conversion is when a person becomes aware that people together are a community, not just an institution, organization, or business. We all form part of an integrated whole, we have specific interrelated roles, we all have gifts needed for the benefit of the whole, and we become our best when we work together for common goals. This first stage of a changed outlook helps us to view everyone else in a different way, to see mission and vision as a shared reality, and to understand that there must be ownership of group values.

The second stage of conversion is when a leader becomes aware of the fact that we are all in this world for a purpose. We must become a part of our world, environment, culture, nation, and even local community. Here, embedded, incarnated in our world is how we live our calling—there is no other way. This leads to consequences towards the environment—namely to protect it; towards our culture—to appreciate it; to our nation—to make decisions that favor it and show responsibility towards it; to our local community—to respond to its needs. We cannot use, abandon, or lay waste all around us—places or people, for profit, but have serious responsibilities.

The third stage of conversion is when a leader comes to grips with the call to service. We are a community, in the heart of this world, and we are here to serve others and our world. This sense of destiny, we are here to serve others—brings forth some of the finest qualities of leadership. These three levels of awareness foster an internal dynamic that leads one to spiritual, servant leadership. Leadership is a form of service rather than service being an effective way to lead. It is easier to be a servant and to learn how to lead than it is to be a leader and then learn how to serve.

6. Appreciate when everything comes together.

As we try to re-discover great leadership and appreciate the importance of a long-term preparation, we know that no transformation takes place without a conversion that leads to a new outlook on life. However, many good qualities can be present in a person's life without moving on to a conversion, often because the moment is not yet right. There are three kinds of time: *tempus* is historical time that measures events, *chronos* is the time that eats away at our lives and consumes us in all kinds of secondary issues, and then there is *kairos* or the special time of grace and blessing. In each person's life there is a "fullness of time," a moment of grace, and a spiritual leader must grasp it when it comes. Transformation takes time and lots of patience. There are many ups and downs in a leader's life, many personal efforts seemingly with no success. All these are not in vain, for there comes a moment when everything comes together, and the leader has no choice but to accept the call. There can be no more delays; this is it—the time to take a new direction in life.

There are many things about leadership that cannot be explained; among them are moments of profound perception that catch up a leader into a new view of reality. It seems a door opens and the leader knows he or she must walk through it to a new appreciation of the vocation of leadership. It is difficult to explain this to someone who has not crossed this threshold. The moment when understandings of one's life, mission, and destiny come into focus happens to people who have prepared well for the transforming impact of the vocation of leadership. Generally at least four aspects of the leader's life need to be well integrated. A leader needs to be knowledgeable about issues and people; can integrate cognitive and emotional aspects of the people and events he or she deals with. Such a leader can make sense out of reality and its, at times, disparate data. Great leaders have this quality, others do not. Second, a leader's own life of intimacy has matured to a point where he or she can trust and benefit from close relationships of friendship and love. This supports the leader in what lies ahead. Third, when everything comes together it is generally when a leader has developed mature adult relationships with those with whom he or she works. Leaders must be able to relate as equals with those around them. It is fine to be the boss as long as one knows the limitations of position and has a healthy give and take with followers. Fourth, a leader who is ready for the moment of insight and transformation must be a person who has clearly defined support systems with friends, family, and peers. Provided a leader's life is mature, then often everything comes together and the leader faces a moment of absolute letting go and accepting the unknown that lies ahead.

7. Choose a good crisis.

When everything in an organization functions smoothly, the only need to maintain such efficiency is good management. People have confidence in the way managers do things and the organization moves along to achieve its pre-established goals. When for one reason or another, things go wrong, followers become concerned, possibly lose confidence, and doubts surface among them. It is time for a reassessment, for a careful analysis of the direction of the organization. We call this moment of judgment a crisis. It is a turning point, at times an explosive crisis that requires the full attention of leadership; day to day management is no longer enough. Often, crisis is not a sudden change of course but a creeping, gradual, deterioration of circumstances. Crisis is now structural and systemic, a normal part of everyday life in organizations. Explosive crises of the past called forth lonely visionaries whose skill and judgment brought speedy resolution to an immediate and critical problem. Today, lonely visionaries cannot answer creeping crises but only leaders who work with communities and respond collaboratively. Leaders do not view crises negatively but rather as opportunities to discern a new direction and bring followers to a new level of maturity.

Facing crises with vision and hope is a major task of a spiritual leader. He or she learns from personal conversion how the call to set a new direction can have healing and life-giving effects on an individual, and facing crises can do the same for an organization. When a leader chooses the right kind of crisis to address, it can draw people to a new level of awareness. It can give insight into shared values and group purpose. It can bring release from the pressures of daily life and enable one to re-establish perspective. It can lead to clarity of judgment on the vision of the organization. Finally, it can give a sense of hope and rekindle awareness of the importance of community.

A leader must deal with all crises that arise; that is what leadership is all about. However, a spiritual leader needs to know when a particular crisis provides an opportunity for organizational transformation. When followers seem dissatisfied and unfulfilled in their work, or give too much time to complaining, or seem to lack energy and enthusiasm for the goals of the organization, a leader should be on the alert. When the institution itself begins to lose its competitive edge and no longer attracts the best applicants, a leader should stop and reassess the situation. When the leader and close associates know they are not as enthusiastic for their common projects as they used to be, a leader must stop the decline. When leaders see themselves, their workers, and the organization's shared goals all weakening at the same time, then this could be a good crisis to choose to address with the full force of a call to conversion and to set a new direction.

8. Set a new direction.

Conversion is essentially a change of the focus of one's mind and heart. It is an awareness that we have lost some of the values we claimed to have and need to set a new direction to be faithful to ourselves. It is not a total re-creating of oneself but a recalling of oneself to one's purpose and destiny. There are three steps in this process—root, interpret, and discover. First, a leader must go back to the foundational roots of his or her life and re-appropriate those rooted values. Second, the leader cannot return in time and stay there, savoring the effective impact values used to have. Rather, he or she must interpret those values for today's changed circumstances. Third, a leader looks to the future and tries to discover how those motivating values can be relevant in new situations that arise in the future. In setting a new direction a leader breaks down the walls that blocked appreciation of past values and breaks open insight and discerns how these values can re-impact the future. Leadership requires a supreme sense of balance. Setting a new direction is not easy. It is a straight and narrow way with many ups and downs. Like climbing a mountain, the leader must be attentive to the goal, take small steps and never overextend oneself, and never turn back. As we have seen it is a journey away from one's weaknesses and towards an increased dedication to others and to values of the Spirit.

This new direction includes the following components. The leader chooses standards and values for their own sake. He or she recognizes gaps in one's own and others' lives and knows they can be transformed. He or she discovers a new courage to accept the difficulties and hardships of being a spiritual leader. As the leader moves forward it is always with others, assuring their acceptance and ownership of all that needs to be done. The leader who sets a new direction is open-minded and open-hearted, seeks input from all, and cherishes alternative solutions. In pursuing this new direction a leader speaks from the heart and fosters a loving community. This path-finding mission brings energy and enthusiasm; it is the prophetical work of leading others to a healing and life-giving future. This is not spectacular leadership, but it is spiritual leadership at its best.

People do not reject leadership but the travesty of leadership that we have suffered from so many. This conversion is a chance to let our practice catch up with where our hearts claim to be. It is an opportunity a spiritual leader never refuses. Such a leader gathers others together in a new way, listens to them intently, shares values and vision, and moves forward energetically and enthusiastically with a shared sense of mission.

9. Pursue ongoing conversion, both personal and organizational.

No thoughtful person is interested in the survival of the fittest, or in leaders who can make what they think are tough decisions. Nowadays, people of spiritual conviction are interested in the survival of the most compassionate, understanding, loving leaders. They maintain their approach to leadership through the ongoing transformation of themselves and their organizations. While we must work at this, God is interested in us and our world and relentlessly pursues us to succeed. Our efforts and God's interventions come in the ordinary events of each day not in exceptional signs and wonders. In conversion a leader learns the truth about himself or herself and knows there is no turning back.

Leaders live out every day the basic insights of their conversional experience, and it becomes a mission in life—to live and make decisions in light of that original experience of conversion. Such a leader tries to utilize basic values and sense of purpose in life so that they form a vision linked to the original conversion. This vision that emerges is who the leader wishes to be, what he or she wishes to do and hopes to achieve, and how he or she can relate to God. A problem that arises with spiritual leaders is that their commitment can become haphazard and episodic. Jesus once commented that people without faith take more care in planning their lives than do people with faith (Luke 16:8). The experience of conversion is an exciting, challenging vision of what we ought to be. If we were to identify the five most important components of this experience what would they be? We know God has endowed us with personal gifts and talents to contribute to this vision that emerges from conversion—what are they? Perhaps we have weaknesses that could stunt our growth—what are they? Let us keep in mind that every gift may well have negative side effects, and every obstacle will have hidden potentialities for good.

However, leaders must take a further step and prudently identify specific goals that help in attaining that vision and develop an action plan to reach desired goals—these are strategies. They are clearly defined steps to implement goals and thus realize the vision that emerges from the experience of conversion. Some will be concrete actions and activities; others will be in-depth reflections and appreciation of new ways of understanding leadership. Then leaders need to know the outcomes they are seeking in each strategy and then assess how successful they are in meeting them. Pursuing ongoing conversion both personal and organizational is a daily commitment that needs to include awareness of the original conversion and then planning to achieve it. Leadership today must be based on spiritual principles; the spiritual values that come with conversion support, enlighten, and give soul to leadership. There will always be ups and downs, stops and restarts, battles won and then re-fought at a deeper level. Conversion is always ongoing, never finished; it is one's daily challenge and sustenance; it is the great guarantee of spiritual leadership.

10. Examine your life constantly.

Spiritual leaders maintain the quality of their commitment by constantly evaluating their lives and leadership. Leadership has four focuses: followers, goals, situation, and the personal call of the leader. Each of these needs evaluating from time to time. Another way of considering the needed evaluation is to consider the topics of each chapter in this book: the notion of leadership, preparations, conversion, call, vision, spirituality, supports, evaluation, and attitudes to followers. There are many ways to examine one's life and leadership and the first is to do it yourself. A leader should always have goals and can personally review these on a regular basis. These goals will focus on the new direction chosen in conversion but will develop into more specific objectives and strategies. At first it is quite appropriate to write down these to aid one's attention. A leader can also facilitate personal evaluation by reflective reading about leadership and the lives of good leaders. Moreover, reflecting on failed leaders and leadership in the daily news can challenge a leader to examine his or her life to see if similar traces of failure are creeping in.

A further aid is to re-examine source values that a leader has always looked to for inspiration and motivation in his or her leadership. This would include the challenges of a religious tradition seen in its Scriptures, history, great figures, and even prayers and poetry. Much of this can inspire, recall values, and bring focus to one's own commitment.

Groups of friends are also an excellent source for examining one's life and leadership. Of course, this requires that they have set up levels of trust, common vision, and shared values, and have maintained an interest in mutual evaluation of commitment. This rarely happens by chance and generally only results from deliberate agreement and organization. Sometimes such groups of friends can be more specific and challenging than are groups of peers. However, the latter are a great source of professional examination and can be more clearly trained to focus on key issues of leadership development.

An important source of reliable professional and personal evaluation is a mentor, someone you trust who can be a sounding board for your values and a source of honest critique of the direction of your life. A mentor is a wise man or woman who speaks the truth to you, gives you advice that you know is good for you, and challenges you when few others will. A mentor becomes a standard of the life you hope to live.

A further component of ongoing examination of a leader's life and values could be this book. You can choose one or other chapter and systematically review the key components of spiritual leadership. We have already seen thirty suggestions in the first three chapters, and many more lie ahead. These can become a detailed program of review to verify if the leader is living the challenges of conversion.

STEP FOUR

ACCEPT THE VOCATION OF LEADERSHIP

When a person dedicates himself or herself to serve others in leadership there results a complete shift in life; it is the moment of call or vocation. In the Hebrew Scriptures every prophet digresses in his teaching to describe the experience he had of being called by God to lead the people. This remembrance of a special experience becomes the prophet's motivation for his life of dedication—he has to lead because he was specifically called to do so. At the same time the call, narrated to others, becomes the authentication and justification for his leadership role. Leaders today need to reflect on their own vocation to serve others; they are set apart, have a God-given destiny, must accept their stature in community, and need to persevere with fidelity.

1. Accept leadership as a vocation.

Men and women of spiritual sensitivity recognize that their leadership is a personal call or vocation in life. Leadership is not the result of mere promotion, although the latter can be a point of departure for a new and deeper perception of one's role in society. Situations of leadership are not the result of blind chance. No one is born to be a leader; rather, there comes a moment when a person realizes he or she is someone or something that he or she was not before, and now has an important role in the service of others.

Some recognize the moment of call in a new job description, in the different way other people relate to them, or in a faith experience. However, the awareness of a vocation to leadership is above all a very personal experience, an appreciation of having a specific and unique task in this world. Awareness of this sense of being called is a powerful impetus to quality leadership.

The vocation to leadership does not refer only to a task and responsibility, but more particularly to a lifestyle; this is at the heart of the vocation—it is a new style of life that results from this new perception of one's role in society. So, the vocation is to Christian leadership, spiritual leadership, servant leadership, and leadership cannot be separated from these inner values. For those who are Christian, this is a fundamental Christian calling, and their leadership cannot be separated from Christ-centered values. Leadership is based on a transformed pattern of life. Some might say it is a call to honesty, integrity, justice, mutual understanding, and love. Others might express the call as a challenge to live the beatitudes, or simply to do more, to love more, and to serve more. This vocation is not a generic call to better living; rather it is a mission specific call to lead others by service. This vocation is a mystery, a gift, a grace, and each one knows he or she must live this call in depth. While it includes responsibility, it is also the result of the initiative of love; it escapes one's understanding, but it seems permeated by love. Perhaps, some will recognize it as a manifestation of the ongoing call to conversion, the challenge to develop to the full the gifts and call experienced in conversion.

This new perception of your life and calling gives you a sense of your irreplaceable role in society. At such a time, you sense you have a real calling in life to do good to others through the vocation of leadership. Now you are at once and in every moment a leader. Such a man or woman experiences a total inability to do anything except give his or her life to the vocation of leadership with all its challenges, responsibilities, pressures, and pain. At the same time, such leaders sense new levels of energy, clarity of purpose, vision, and space for liberty and originality. Think of the consequences of your refusal.

2. Journey inward to identify your destiny.

So many people in leadership positions today are socially irresponsible. However, there are increasing numbers who want to be socially responsible. Their leadership is affected by awareness of their call and by the quality of their spiritual lives. Nowadays, one finds quality leadership in men and women who can maintain in dynamic tension their management and leadership skills with values of the spirit. They are not embarrassed to acknowledge the overlapping of two worlds. Such leaders appreciate the basic values that motivate their lives. Out of these values comes an awareness of an enduring purpose in life, and this leads one to appreciate one's destiny in this world—a destiny to be a transformed, spiritual leader. This sense of one's identity results from the inward journey into one's heart to discover one's hopes, dreams, and calling. It includes the capacity to be alone in contemplative reflection and quietly discover one's identity and place in life. This then grows and evolves over time into an appreciation of one's leadership calling.

At times we are too busy living to fully understand our lives. However, this inward journey of self-discovery helps us transcend our perceived limitations, challenges us to get away from surface problems, and impels us to thirst to be more than we have ever been. Great leaders are all grounded in values of the spirit, as they search for meaning in life and their role in it. So, spiritual leadership is a choice for personal identity—who one wants to be, what kind of a leader one chooses to be. It speaks about how one sees one's own meaning and purpose in life. This inward journey pushes one's conversion to new depths, integration, and connectedness; it is a personal pilgrimage to mature into one's true self, that one and only way that is particular to oneself and one's leadership.

This inward journey to identify one's destiny gives one tremendous energy to respond as a transformed leader, inspired to serve others, and feel it is all worthwhile. One lives from the inner spiritual core out to others with a personal style of leadership. Above all, one knows one is called and placed among others with a vocation to serve; one might be marginal to common trends in the world, but one accepts this vocation as the only way to be one's true self. A leader who makes this inward journey must have inner peace, then acts on what he or she believes with personal integrity. Such a person walks unhesitatingly according to his or her vocation with living faith, inspiring hope, and loving service.

This deepening appreciation of one's call includes acceptance of one's gifts and mission. Such a leader accepts his or her role and stature, even realizing he or she is a gift for others. This is part of a fascinating and frightening mystery, and a leader must have the courage to be a person of hope. This inward journey is the very personal discovery of one's identity and destiny, but the resulting awareness is that all leadership is with and for others in community. The experience makes one what he or she should be and calls one to fearlessly accept the wholeness of God's gifts, perceiving that leadership is the expression of one's charisms.

3. Maintain a sense of humility.

Corruption, greed, and addiction to power and control over others ooze from the pseudo-leadership of so many contemporary leaders, most of who actually think they are virtuous. And yet, it is clear to anyone who studies Jesus' life in the Scriptures that Christian leadership is not based on power but on humility. This is a new model, a totally different way of thinking about leadership. This is the leadership of those who are aware of their vocation— they know they have not earned their leadership; it has been given to them. Unfortunately, so many go through life today convinced that leadership is power. Such superficial individuals fail to grasp the ultimate meaning of life or their own true destiny within the context of human development. There is no role in leadership today for arrogant, narcissistic people who emphasize their own self-importance, status, prestige, and power. One great mistake is at the root of all failed leadership—pride, and its constant focusing on self.

It is frequently the case that a leader has a place of honor in community, and he or she usually exceeds followers in many areas of organizational life with its interpersonal and task oriented skills. But such leaders should not exaggerate their own importance but rather insist on having received these gifts from God. We have already seen that leadership is ultimately what God is doing in and through us. So, being a leader implies self-surrender, interpreting one's meaning in life in the broader context of God's gifts. Being able to appreciate the mystery of life and leadership as gifts helps one to be humble, to be one's authentic self, to honestly know one's strengths and weaknesses, and to engender genuine respect for others and their gifts.

Humility in leadership is a recognition of one's humanity and place in community. We are not in this world for our personal enhancement but to live and grow in solidarity with others. We are all struggling and striving to grow, and equally share in a spirituality of failure just as much as in one of mutual enrichment. Even in our personal spiritual journey we can give ourselves permission to be less than perfect, as we experience insecurity, failure, and poverty. Humility gives us the ability to bounce back, try again, experiment with fresh ideas, and stand up to resistance. Humility helps us have faith, hope, and love in God, in others, and in ourselves. Often there is more wisdom and courage in dealing humbly with failure than in expecting success all the time. Moreover, we learn so much in our humility that can help us in dealing with others. This is the paradox of leadership that our failures become successes, our weaknesses become strengths, and our own pain can teach us how to heal others.

Humility will teach you to appreciate others, to be more accountable, to keep a just perspective on efforts and results. It teaches you never to judge others without first judging yourself. Humility reminds you not to belittle others, or criticize them, or to fail to give others your undivided attention. It insists you should not be pre-occupied with yourself, to play favorites with others, to make distinctions based on status, or to embarrass people around us. Above all humility teaches you to trust others, to practice integrity, to be open to improvement, and to be sincere in everything you do.

4. Do no harm as a leader.

We all know that physicians take an oath to do no harm, and this precedes all their efforts to bring healing to their patients. As we have seen the recent disastrous harm done by some leaders, we can only wish that they, too, would take the oath to do no harm.

Unfortunately, we have seen so many bad leadership decisions that it has been common to consider that many people in leadership positions in our generation have done more harm than good. Only those with the vision and dedication of spiritual leaders can reverse this trend and stop this decay. As a spiritual leader it is a critical component of call that you do no harm, that you do not let others responsible to you do harm, that you do not allow your organization do harm, and that you assure that your products and services do no harm. Leadership is an attitude of service, and it begins by pledging to do no harm.

On a personal level a spiritual leader must remove from his or her life all negative influences, the slow erosion of values, and the corrupting influence of power that do harm to others. He or she must remove arrogance, deceit, and any harmful trait. A leader avoids hiding in creative ignorance, checks his or her addictions, and makes conscious those areas of personal life that need healing. All these personal defects can harm others.

Great leaders have system skills, the ability to see how every person fits into an organization and has an important role to play. So, a spiritual leader never belittles others and their contributions, ends destructive and confrontational positions, as well as neglect of workers, turf wars, coercion of followers, harassment, and using people. He or she stops the harmful effects of disharmony, confusing expectations, excessive internal competition, infighting, unhealthy comparisons, petty jealousies, mutual blame, compromising integrity, unethical practices, and lack of mutual love. He or she makes sure there is no stunting of others' development and no one is enslaved to any aspect of organizational life. When a leader removes harm from other people's lives he or she achieves a lot.

A spiritual leader checks any controlling and harmful influences within the organization. He or she removes the dysfunctional aspects of the organization—restricting communication, misusing power, unjust salary scales, and careerism. A spiritual leader will be on the lookout for those controlling influences in organizations, large or small, that do harm whether one wants it or not. Often memories harm when people remember how they were badly treated. These unhealed hurts delete a sense of hope among workers. Sometimes a spiritual leader sees harm and cannot respond when it comes from others. However, in such cases a spiritual leader will not participate so as not to encourage such behavior.

Doing no harm is a first step for a leader who must remove harm while appreciating potential harm is best dealt with proactively by creating a healthy atmosphere between leaders and workers—listening, maintaining high values, respect, admiration, total acceptance of others with their strengths and weaknesses. Many challenges lie ahead for you as a spiritual leader but quality leadership begins with a serious dedication to do no harm.

5. Realize you are called to be nothing less than a leader.

This book focuses exclusively on the personal development of a spiritual leader. So far we have seen it needs reflection, extended preparations, transforming conversion, and a profound sensitivity and awareness of one's vocation to leadership. We are not interested in anything less than the call to be a great leader, and this is not an easy journey. Responding to this call is first and foremost a dynamic process of constant change and growth. Part of this process is the acceptance of a hierarchy of moral and spiritual values and a dedication never to accept a reduced ideal of this calling. This process of responding to call includes a constant dimension of enriched inter-relationships between leader and followers that are mutually influential, and filled with mutual respect and awareness of mutual dependence. Leadership is a serious commitment and demands skills—including an openness to keep learning, a fostering of new ideas, and a re-education of the imagination. Furthermore, this call includes an awareness that power is always shared with others—an approach that calls for new skills. This power needs to be linked to wisdom, one without the other serves little for a leader. Finally, as we have seen, leadership development depends on a discovery of one's inner self and values—a change of heart and mind.

Through this process of conversion and response to call a person begins to become a spiritual leader. Such a person needs to be at peace with himself or herself and strong enough to accept the new public stature that results. The leader needs to be humble, while giving strength to others; to be a hundred percent involved while protecting oneself from burnout. It is a total commitment that leads to improved quality life on personal, family, and friendship levels as well as organizational. This commitment means living in tension between the current status and a better changed situation. So, the leader must cope with resistance and do so with courageous perseverance and hope-filled confidence.

This kind of leader finds motivation and direction in his or her vision of faith. The leader is essentially a visionary and an experienced mediator between this world's needs and the challenges of a world beyond. So, the leader is a guide to open a new way forward, to sow seeds of a new way of human interaction, and to inspire and challenge others to rethink their approach to life. The leader ploughs ahead to make this vision concrete and specific, willingly making adaptations when necessary, but never compromising values. These leaders are examples of the transformative spiritual values they cherish.

The call to be a great leader means being a magnanimous person of truthfulness and integrity who can break down barriers and release the potential of followers. We could call this adult leadership, and it requires passion, boldness, and courage. This leadership is not haphazard or episodic but is a fundamental choice to be a person for others; to be a person of optimism, enthusiasm, inspiration, and influence; to be a leader who can discern others' charisms, give them a sense of authority and direction, and urge them to relentless dedication to a shared vision. The call we are discussing in this chapter is a powerful invitation to become a significant person in community. It is not for the weak-hearted or partially identified. It is a way of life. The person who accepts this call will never be the same again, and neither will the people with whom he or she works, lives, and shares life.

6. Nourish the call of leadership.

In a later chapter we will consider the spirituality and supports needed to maintain commitment to spiritual leadership. However, even from the initial conversion and awareness of call one must nourish this vocation to leadership. The leader must awaken the life of the spirit which will assure him or her of freedom and on-going renewal that will extend the call and will be an antidote to leadership obsolescence. Here are a few simple suggestions as initial nourishment of call. First, the leader should take care of self, physically as well as spiritually. The initial enthusiasm to give oneself totally to respond to the call must not damage one's sense of wholeness and health. The leader should also focus on self, family life, and friendships; he or she should keep a healthy self-concept, a life of intimacy and friendship, and enjoy the beautiful experiences of life.

Second, each one should remember the chosen path of leadership and keep on it. The vocation to give one's life in service of others is the reason for all we do. This calls for purity of motives, doing things because they are right and not for any reward. This can become difficult in a world that is unsympathetic to the values of the spirit. The leader has something to say, a mission to accomplish, and must not give up in this task of the remaking of leadership. As one remembers one should cultivate gratitude for this extraordinary calling.

Third, a leader should maintain commitment to the chosen spiritual values that can raise the moral and spiritual motivation of all around. A leader can win over others, motivate and mobilize them with higher ideals. Maintaining these values requires intellectual fortitude and personal integrity. Such leaders will need to live with uncertainty, as they look for new ways to implement their values. They will need to come up with creative solutions in spite of surrounding limitations. Maintaining values is a leader's prophetic task of enlightenment and discovery.

Fourth, a leader keeps in touch with those around, treating them with appreciation and friendship. A leader works from shared values to deeper shared values, and this implies reexamining one's beliefs about community, focusing on growth with and through others. It means a life of compassion, listening, group cohesiveness, communication, that leads to a sense of communion from which follows motivation and mobilization of others. Leaders who hope to do this need to keep close to others, be fair and honest, be respectful and generous, and show confidence and trust.

Fifth, a spiritual leader keeps an eye on the future, for this is where hopes will be realized. It means being a constant learner, envisioning solutions never tried before, using new criteria, discovering new ways to be a leader. Leaders must have faith in the power of their vision, be creative in the way they make decisions, maintain several alternatives for discussion, build bridges to people and their ideas, and constantly tap the gifts of others.

Sixth, a leader should recognize the extraordinary in the ordinary events of each day. Turning a blind eye to the extraordinary when we see it makes us blind. Leaders need to be modern mystics who can experience a sense of mystery in life, share it, and explain its consequences to others. They can constantly interrupt business as usual in the so-called real world and draw attention to connections to values of a world beyond this one.

7. Recognize you are called to love.

Spiritual leaders insist that people and relationships precede structures and tasks. This implies leaders need to think positively of others, try to understand them, forgive when necessary, and always show compassion. After all, the journey to spiritual leadership begins with an awareness of being loved, not with the leader's love for others. The latter follows on the former and is a response to the call to leadership. It is a journey in which the leader daily makes decisions based on love. Thus, he or she changes attitudes to life, rejecting selfishness, greed, self-satisfaction, and thus moves away from self-centeredness to the service of others. Appreciating that one can transform leadership with love is a rigorous self-training. When a leader is motivated by a conviction of the transforming value of love, he or she treats others with a natural benevolence, wishes them well before any encounter, appreciates the good in others, and presumes that they will do good. This positive, optimistic approach to others has a healing effect on relationships and opens up the development of a different kind of leadership. Loving and encouraging approaches are more effective than adversarial ones and give the leader far more ability to influence others and draw the best out of them. In such an environment followers sense they are loved and grow as individuals and then contribute more to the common vision and mission.

When a leader focuses on the love of others in daily life, he or she emphasizes simple human qualities that are also a noble part of being human—attitudes that are humanizing, caring, trusting, and supportive. Focusing on others requires tolerance of their differences, dialogue, forgiveness, and reconciliation. It means mutual respect, appreciation of each other's gifts and genuine solidarity. A leader can do so much good to others by allowing them to be themselves, living in interdependence and mutual esteem. For such a leader the welfare of others is as important as one's own. This includes concern for others' health and well-being, both material and spiritual. Engaging in the welfare of others calls the leader to delight in others' growth and advancement, furthering their rights, protecting their justice, and celebrating their achievements and progress.

A spiritual leader who recognizes that he or she is called to love makes a positive difference to other people's lives by respecting their dignity, empowering them in whatever ways possible, thus releasing their human energy, talent, and dedication. A spiritual leader can look into others' hearts. Such a leader does not impose views, vision, or priorities, but influences others to be the best they are capable of being. Part of that response will be to help others appreciate their own basic values, enduring purpose, and mission in life. The leader can also train others to be visionaries; helping them to see what others do not, but also challenging them to look at things in a different way. This requires understanding, building connections, giving visibility and significant responsibilities to others, collaborating, challenging constructively, and working toward shared values and mission. Recognizing that one is called to love has serious consequences, for love is very practical and demanding on a leader at every moment of each day.

8. Be the best you can be.

As a leader you need to be aware that other people depend on you, they need you to be your best, passionate about your leadership, and totally given in service to others. Managing well is not enough; you must inspire and motivate others to also be their best, to deepen a sense of meaning in their lives. You will need enthusiasm, courage, confidence, and generosity. Others will need to know you are trustworthy, decisive, ready to learn, and have their interests at heart. You do not need to be perfect—no one is, but you need to be the best you can be in whatever situation presents itself. Your task is to lead, and that means reinventing yourself as situations change and new challenges arise, for you must not only lead today but be ready for tomorrow. You must prove each day that you are a spiritual leader, a servant leader, motivated by values of the spirit, nurtured in reflection, and authenticated in the authority of your spiritual life.

To strive to be your best is a daily challenge, the touchstone of a dedicated call; it is a commitment that can never be laid aside. This means discerning carefully what is the optimum way of living your leadership. You are called to be the best you can be—not just the best for you and your own maturity, but also the best for all those involved. This means making choices that provide hope but imply risk, choices that require a process of discernment. Such a process begins with identifying alternative responses to an issue that requires a decision, weighing the pros and cons of each alternative, seeking freedom of spirit in evaluating each option, praying for guidance, involving the input of others especially those affected by the decision, identifying which response does the most good, and then making the decision with firmness and peace.

What constitutes the best you can do and be? You must explicitly pursue the mission of the institution and evidence dedication to the group's shared values. What you do should give you a sense of accomplishment in your leadership, a feeling of doing the right thing. It should also positively contribute to co-workers and to clients and customers. In small or significant ways your decisions and your work should positively affect others, changing their lives for the better. What you do must always be the most loving thing to do in any given situation.

Leaders who appreciate they are called to be the best they can be make judgments in fidelity to their call. This habit of mind to make conscious choices based on one's call is central to spiritual leadership. It will involve wrestling with contradictions as one struggles to stay in touch with the realities of daily organizational life and the realities of one's call. It means maintaining high hopes amidst mini despairs, as one seeks to build the moral and spiritual renewal of the organization. It implies the ability to live with ambiguity sometimes never knowing if one's decisions have any results.

9. Maintain the dream.

Part of a leader's calling is to be the source of a dream that attracts others. One's scope as a leader has widened, giving one a new freedom to be what one has always dreamed of being and at the same time, little by little, to also help others to dream. When we seem to live with global burnout and people are depressed with their leaders, institutions, and hopes for the future, maintaining a dream is more important than ever.

The dream a spiritual leader promotes is that people can achieve personal fulfillment and can build community together. Working together in dialogue, collaboration, and dynamic relationships, we can enrich each other and in synergy achieve more together than as separate parts. We can dream of uniting work and spirituality, believing we can do good while working well, and thus that we can contribute to the common good. In contemporary organizations with their tensions and pressures, a leader can still foster high morale. The dream reminds us that all people are important for who they are and not for the kind of work they do. A leader can create an environment that is conducive to human growth and spiritual maturity.

It is the leader's task to draw others to the dream. This includes building positive attitudes from inside the organization and not being put off by inevitable criticisms. It starts by challenging old ways and showing the benefits of change and transformation. A leader does this by sharing information and insights, and by raising issues no one else does. It means sharing your thinking even if it unsettles and disturbs others. At the same time a leader shares knowledge, he or she must share on an affective level, empathizing with others, and letting them know they are loved. The leader must evidence enthusiasm and excitement for the dream and inspire confidence that together people can attain it. He or she needs to be optimistic, constantly joyful, and always ready to celebrate intermediate achievements on the journey to the dream. Maintaining a dream is a sign of leadership maturity and calls the leader to set high attainable goals, to teach all the time, and to share and learn from others. A spiritual leader is a dreamer who offers refreshing and creative ideas and longs to communicate his or her dream, ideas, vision, and intuitions with others. There is a magical property about leadership as the leader enables others to dream.

10. Value gift, acceptance, and receptivity.

Call is a gift and so essentially emphasizes receptivity. Certainly, leadership consists in achievement and attaining of goals, but for spiritual leaders there is always the additional dimensions of acceptance and receptivity. Spiritual leaders become experts in a different kind of learning, a genuine wisdom that enables them to appreciate how much they gain from the gift of leadership and from the support, talents, and competencies of others. A spiritual leader discovers his or her greater self in community with others. This means a spiritual leader must emphasize new perspectives on leadership, appreciating others' vocations, searching for enrichment in diversity, identifying creative non-traditional thinking, and fostering a caring environment that enables integration of others and their contributions. Call is a gift that draws the best out of you, and you can do the same for others. A good spiritual leader is always restless until he or she brings together the gifts of others. Awareness that one can achieve much more by receiving than by personal achievement alone becomes a new kind of motivational power in a group and brings new vitality into the group's interactions.

Appreciating that life, call and leadership are gifts implies a profound discovery of enrichment through passivity. Spiritual maturity has two phases—one active when a person does everything and one passive when a person finds that some things happen to him or her that one must receive with humility and gratitude. Exaggerated activity is a sign of an early stage in leadership, and passivity and receptivity are indications of a more mature stage in one's leadership development.

Awareness and acceptance of the gift of a call to leadership makes one sensitive to the joy and beauty of reception; that one can accomplish much because of what one has been given. These gifts along with support and guidance of others helps one realize what one can do for others and what others can do. Acceptance of gift makes one aware that each leader is a gift for others, and with this comes the realization that everyone is also gifted in one way or another.

A spiritual leader who appreciates his or her gifts cultivates a sense of awe and wonder, and acknowledges that there are two horizons to life—this one with its challenges and a realm beyond this from which the call comes. Such a leader can rejoice in hope, immerse self in compassion, persevere with a sense of mission, and appreciate the importance of gratitude in prayer. Such a leader should register how he or she feels, knowing others will feel similar when the leader generously calls and offers gifts of acceptance and challenge. Sharing with others helps them understand what leadership means—it is a gift. Acceptance of call reminds a leader that we are a charismatic community, at our best when we share gifts for the common good. So, this receptivity leads to new priorities and values, to a more holistic approach to leadership.

STEP FIVE

IMPLEMENT YOUR CALL IN A VISION

After decades of failed leadership when many seemed content to be condemned to ordinary or even superficial leadership, we now face distinct possibilities of a rebirth of outstanding leadership in our generation. Many men and women are deciding what really matters for them in life and in leadership and are willing to confront the new realities of leadership with a sense of vocation and call. These people will undoubtedly be leaders of action, but they also know that action without vision is merely passing time. Helen Keller was once asked if there was anything worse than being blind. She replied that there was—a person with sight and no vision. Spiritual leaders know they must seriously engage the failures of recent years, re-define leadership as a vision of hope, and interpret their mission in light of the future. These leaders will be known for their truthfulness, trustfulness, and compassionate care. They will be people of contemplative reflection, everyday inspiration, broad-based participation, and open communication. They must carefully prepare their followers for transition, letting go of old ways, burning off arrogance and greed, seeking better values, journeying towards vision, and always involved in the most loving thing to do. More than anything else they must implement their call in a vision.

1. Recognize the pre-requisites of vision.

Preparing oneself and others for dedication to a newly discovered vision cannot be separated from a leader's personal values in life, from what drives the leader, from that which he or she believes. These basic values find expression in an enduring purpose in life, the reason why one is here, the expression of who a person is—that distinguishes the person from everyone else. These basic values, together with the enduring purpose, form a leader's philosophy of life, and from this flows a sense of mission and destiny. These pre-requisites must be permeated with integrity, credibility, and trust. Followers need to know that leaders will be true to themselves and to the vision they proclaim. The leader who wishes to pursue a shared vision with the group will need courage to speak the values he or she pursues, to present ideas with humility, and to appreciate one's need of others' views. Such a leader will need intellectual honest, consistency in dealing with others, ability to handle differences and conflict, and the gift to handle all with inner peace. One of the most important qualities for one who wants to establish a shared vision will be the building of a trusting environment. Trust will be the emotional glue that binds a group together in a shared vision.

Among the many pre-requisites for leadership, there are six key requirements in a leader's preparation for visioning. First, a leader makes co-workers aware of their dignity and responsibility. This means the leader needs to learn more about all employees and to let them know that he or she appreciates their gifts and contributions to the organization. This will imply allowing and even fostering creativity, loosening controls so that workers feel free to take risks, giving guidance when necessary, and celebrating successes. Second, a leader who wishes to prepare followers to establish a shared vision must help them welcome change whenever it occurs. This includes dealing with the emotional aspects of change, overcoming resistance to change, and encouraging followers to appreciate the growth that can come through change. Third, a leader must initiate preparatory training to ready followers for a new vision. So, the leader will give others time to understand and buy into the vision, communicating well and endeavoring to surface new ideas in followers, helping them anticipate problems and be proactive, and using collaborative styles for learning, sharing, consulting, goal-setting, and strategic planning.

Fourth, a leader must coach his or her followers by giving them important work to do, allowing them discretion in it, providing them with visibility and recognition, and evaluating together. Fifth, a leader understands that a pre-requisite for authentic shared vision is collaboration that leads to participation in decision-making. Workers will not participate unless they have ownership of decisions, plans, and shared vision. Collaboration requires mutual respect, peace, freedom of spirit, reflection, discernment, and courage. Eventually collaboration needs to take place on three levels: intellectual, organizational, and personal. Sixth, a leader who wants to establish a shared vision needs to treat workers as partners. The best run organizations treat followers as adults. This means leader and followers trust, communicate, care, serve each other, draw the best out of each other, tap each other's gifts, and reflect together.

2. Identify the components of a vision.

For a leader to have vision several components are necessary. First, vision is the art of seeing what others do not yet see or maybe do not yet want to see. This is an aspect of wisdom that includes appreciating people's hopes, society's future needs, obstacles that could arise, who are the key players, and how to unite diverse contributions for the attaining of a common goal. Vision is the ability to see the big picture. Therefore, the leader must see all sides of an issue, strengths and weakness in followers' perceptions, and have the gift of analyzing short term and long term perspectives. Vision means also seeing the overarching picture—how hopes, activities, and decisions in the present relate to values of a world beyond this one. Second, vision is not only seeing what others do not see, but deliberately looking at things in ways others do not. This attentive perception means constant discernment and evaluation in light of basic personal values and implies searching for ways of articulating one's enduring purpose in life. This is part of a leader's constant passion to move from what is to what ought to be. He or she looks at reality from the perspective of God's plan for the world—this is true vision. Third, vision is the ability to see, to look, and to then ask why? A leader must know the "why" of each decision. So, a leader looks at situations in order to integrate personal and organizational vision and to make decisions that generate ownership and manifest organizational charism. Fourth, vision is freely chosen after considering consequences; it is a pattern of life. Vision is faith in action, and even more it is a choice made with and for others, to involve others in the creation of a desirable future.

What are the components of a good vision? 1. A vision must embody one's basic personal values. It is impossible to have a vision that is disconnected from the motivating values of one's life. All should be able to recognize themselves in the shared vision. 2. Vision must be genuinely shared. The process of creating a vision must include the imagination of the whole group. Vision belongs to everyone, and a leader must presume that others contribute to the shared vision. 3. Vision must inspire and motivate all who share it. It offers something great that people can yearn for, strive for, and find satisfaction and fulfillment when they attain it. 4. Vision pushes and stretches people to be their greater selves, draws the best out of people, amazes them that they can do things they never thought they could. Thus, it calls for new ideas, tolerates failure without reprimand, encourages risk taking, and leads to breakthrough futures. 5. Vision calls for hope—the primary motivator of exceptional leadership. Vision with hope can transform the world. A leader can have many plans and commitments, but it is a vision of hope that keeps the leader engaged and dedicated. 6. Vision is a response to people's yearnings for a better future. It is an answer to local needs. Followers grasp the vision, understand it, and resonate with its challenge. Vision is an expression of common identity and empowers everyone in its attainment. 7. Vision is never fixed or unchanging, but evolves with others' ongoing questions, clarifications, and responses to new needs. Vision demands constant assessment, new meanings and expectations, and new creative formulations. 8. Vision prepares for the future on personal, community, and organizational levels. It facilitates a breakthrough to new approaches to organizational growth. Vision is how you look at things, how you think, how you respond to the future, how you see followers' interactivity as community, and how you plan.

3. Repair the past.

Vision relates primarily to the future and then to the present in so far as a spiritual leader makes present decisions in light of future hopes. However, it is not possible to construct a shared vision on defective foundations from the past. Harm has often been done to others by former visionless leaders, and that needs to be healed. Harm has often been done to the integrity and trustworthiness of an organization, and that needs to be undone. Sometimes the harm ends but the roots of evil are deep and a spiritual leader must dig out the evils of the past before moving forward. Some organizational evils—such as the greed and the lack of ethics we have seen—take such a hold there is not much one can do but cut out the cancer before moving ahead. Thus, not only does vision impact the future but it must also heal the past. Visionary leaders often live in pain, when they confront the decay of an organization's values, or see how co-workers have surrendered to mediocrity regarding the quality of their commitment. If transformative change is to occur everyone must take responsibility for the reform of structures and of the values of their organization; they must together raise up the shared vision and give birth to a new dawn.

A spiritual leader repairs the past in several ways. Before anything else a leader must humbly review his or her own life to identify serious or smaller failures that have done harm and may continue to do so. Perhaps the first question a person in a leadership position should ask is whether he or she is suitable as a leader. The best service some can perform for their organizations is to leave them. In examining one's own past in need of repair, an honest leader may identify negative attitudes to people, abusive misuses of the organization for one's own benefits, a lack of direction, a failure to build community, an awareness of being distrusted, disliked, and disapproved of. Sometimes, a friend or mentor, a peer in another organization, or a spouse, can pinpoint obvious defects that a leader fails to see.

A spiritual leader must repair harm done to others either by former leaders or by the organization's unhealthy structures or policies. Every organization has people in pain for one reason or another, and before a leader can move forward to vision, he or she must restore others to they can give their best. This means attention to a healthy working environment, just policies, and open communications. It also calls for the removal of any unethical practices, misuse of power, unjust salary scales, and autocratic administration. Spiritual leaders will build a spirit of reconciliation, mutual appreciation, and a strong sense of community.

A spiritual leader will need to give attention to repairing damage done by the organization itself, perhaps because of its lack of shared values, vision, and mission. He or she will check the structural components—value statement, strategic plan, code of ethics, oversight board, hiring procedures, decision-making processes, and conflict management procedures. Only when the organization functions to the benefit of workers can the leader move forward to vision.

4. Be a servant-spiritual leader.

Today's vision of leadership is a self-defining choice, a renewed focus on what is truly important in life. For a spiritual leader vision starts with a rediscovery of a sense of call to serve others—everything else follows from this. A leader who has pondered the nature of leadership, prepared well, accepted the challenge of conversion, and become aware of being personally called, senses that the transformative leadership for which he or she strives is essentially a matter of service, care of others, compassionate responsibility, and selfless love. Such a leader has crossed a threshold to an awareness that the whole of his or her life and destiny center on being a servant leader. The call is identical to vision that empowers and enables such individuals to give themselves to the service of others; it is an awakening to a vision of servant leadership that will permit no interference, it demands an unyielding response in respect and love. Such a leader is convinced that unimaginable results of leadership can be achieved when linked to service. This is not fantasy; it is a fresh vision of the vocation of leadership.

Such leadership has its own program of action. It starts with dedicated service, honest vulnerability, and inner integrity. It requires that the leader constantly give example of the vision, coach and guide others in its values, and create a climate of mutual trust. Servant leadership means giving priority to others and not to oneself, influencing others to be visionaries, and fostering self-leadership in followers. Spiritual leaders of this conviction are honest and reliable in moments of truth. They inspire commitment in others to a shared vision, show love, encouragement, and care for their followers. They can criticize constructively, bear the pain involved in leadership, and generate enthusiasm among followers for the vision they share. Shifting the focus from self to others is the task of the spiritual leader, and this service lifts the spirit of everyone. His or her responsibility is to facilitate the growth of others through leadership. This kind of leader shares responsibility collegially, encourages others to share their knowledge, and appreciates that organizations need to become more democratic. This approach stimulates self-leadership in followers, integrates some feminine characteristics of leadership, and envisions a percolating model of leadership and not an exclusively top-down approach.

To be a servant leader requires that you always behave in ways that are consistent with the values of servant leadership, giving credit to others whenever possible, listening appreciatively to followers, and establishing their ownership for everything you do. To be such a leader means at times that you leave decision-making to others, get out of their way, and celebrate their successes. Being a spiritual servant leader is a way of life—a vision of who you are called to be. Each day you must do something to be a servant leader—just do it!

5. Develop the skills for visioning.

Implementing one's personal call or the organization's call in a vision requires specific leadership skills. On a personal level the leader needs foresight, planning and strategic skills. The leader is not only forward looking but needs to inspire others to join him or her in looking to the future vision. The leader needs a spirit of youthfulness and excitement linked to the wisdom of age;

confidence in the value of the future vision without arrogance that imposes one's views. The leader imagines the vision in action before implementing it. He or she should be a dreamer and encourage others to dream too; a prophet who also trains and encourages others to be prophetical. Called to serve the vision, the leader creates interruptions in the ways things have always been done and launches out to new alternative possibilities. In doing so, he or she must constantly ask questions no one else does and adapt, adjust, and redirect the vision as needed.

Creativity for the future most frequently comes from the grassroots of an organization rather than from the establishment, so a leader focuses on facilitating followers' involvement. The leader asks, how can I give opportunities to learn, while allowing some risk-tasking and failure without reprimand? He or she emphasizes community building and synergetic growth. Along these lines a leader also facilitates emotional and volitional development, so people become willing to change, to accept transition, to share, and to sacrifice for the common good. In this sense the leader tries to unlock the potentials of the heart, facilitate spiritual development, and even include poetic and artistic appreciation as ways of fostering new intuitive ways of thinking, discovering, and visioning. Among followers a good spiritual leader creates working conditions that facilitate creative interactions and a culture of innovation. He or she fosters a discussion of great ideas that unite, a broad human consciousness that makes people big hearted and big minded, and a social imagination that enables a world consciousness.

In developing the skills of visioning a leader needs to be aware that contributing to the common good is part of developing one's own life. However, the focus is different; a spiritual leader always wants to be faithful to the vision of promise and so focuses not on what is but rather more on what ought to be. This means cultivating a sense of mystery and awe and encouraging followers to foster an alternative consciousness that organizations and their work must be and can be different. Sometimes this is nothing more than making conscious what already lies unconscious in followers. Leaders who wish to move followers to the future need to think, reflect, and contemplate, for out of such reflection comes the skill to create new skills of thinking outside conventional categories, beyond traditional boundaries, and out to new horizons. The spiritual leader, while focused on the future, reviews past events that gave birth to dangerous memories—those past events that gave remarkable insight into human interaction and cannot be ignored. The leader must also confront the future with courage and even "create dangerously" (Camus).

6. Be a leader of hope.

Hope is the key motivating factor of a leader's life. Leaders of hope constantly search for the connection between doing a good job in the present and being faithful to the vision of promise that comes from hope. Hope tells the leader who we are called to be and how we are challenged to live in light of the future in which he or she believes and hopes. Hope is a leader's conviction, a vision of what the future should be like, a new and greater reality to which we are being drawn. In all daily efforts a leader cannot reconcile with what he or she sees but only with what he or she hopes to achieve as part of the vision of God for humanity. For such a person hope is the source of life, as it is the source of leadership. The spiritual leader is motivated by values deep within his or her heart, and these values come from a vision of hope for humanity that includes community, mutuality, justice, integrity, and personal and communal fulfillment. In showing us what it means to be truly human, hope informs us how we should live in the present.

When a leader has a vision of hope in self and in others, there follows a series of attitudes the leader employs to bring about this vision. Such leaders trust others profoundly and seek to awaken them to their calling. They support others, affirm them, and appreciate their contribution to the shared vision. The leader sustains hope in followers by inspiring them, thus giving them energy, a sense of well-being, encouragement, and challenge to be their best and to realize their own hopes. A leader of hope focuses on the vision by calling followers to make choices that are significant for the realization of the vision—not easy choices but the hard ones that construct the desired future. A leader of hope calls followers to be courageous and determined; to take risks and to dare do what hope calls for, daring to believe the future can become reality. A spiritual leader identifies others' gifts that contribute to the vision of hope and empowers them to use their gifts to bring about the hoped-for vision. A leader who has hope not only in the vision but also in followers' contributions to the vision delegates authority and significant responsibilities to others, for the vision is one of cooperation, collaboration, mutuality, and community. Finally, the leader called to hope celebrates followers' successes. This may well relate to what has been achieved, but more importantly it creates attitudes that motivate people to look to the future in hope. Celebrations look to the past and anticipate the future in hope.

Leadership means moving people to a better future—it emerges from hope and generates hope. All great leaders are men and women of hope, and they fill others with enthusiasm born of their conviction in a vision of hope. Hope includes struggles for a leader, as it calls for the abandoning of the false securities of the past and a journey to the unknown. However, it is not a journey to make alone but includes others of similar vision, companions of hope.

7. Foster habits of mind and heart.

Practice centeredness. We live in a distracting world where we are bombarded by information, suggestions, novelty, and consumerism at all times. A spiritual leader needs to develop the habit of centering life, or finding that quiet central point of one's life, that zone where true vision, insight, and clarity lie. This is a form of recollection; we re-collect our thoughts on what is important. It is a process of concentration in silence and simplification in the midst of complexity, in which all secondary issues fade out of focus, and the leader is left with clarity of direction. This includes reviewing all the pros and cons of an issue, selecting, choosing, and discerning priorities, coming face to face with what are the overridingly important issues in the pursuit of vision.

Focus on spirituality. Spirituality is the desire to become our true selves, our best selves. It constantly stresses what I am giving to this life and what I am getting out of it. It refers to the pursuit of life within the context of ultimate realities that give meaning to life. For a leader it means the habit of daily engagement motivated by core values that come from within, in what we often call the life of the spirit. The spiritual leader never forgets his or her conversion and call to become a person of interiority. Such a leader is never afraid to speak about what truly motivates life, the values of God's vision for human community. For the contemporary spiritual leader the focus on spirituality is integral to effective leadership.

Be truthful. A spiritual leader must be wise enough to be truthful at all times. Clearly, untruthfulness is damaging to leadership, but so too is a lack of full disclosure and complete communication. A leader must be truthful in the pursuit of a shared vision, never compromising on values, never watering down the goals. But he or she needs to appreciate that truthfulness is not owned, it is found with and through others. This appreciation helps a leader to be clear about his or her place in the world, even his or her stature. At the same time, part of truthfulness is not to live an artificial life, claiming unreal privilege, but humbly and objectively to see similarities between oneself and others. The leader acquires the habit of being truthful at all times in life and practices.

Share. The vision of a spiritual leader can only be maintained when aided by the habit of sharing, which is part of the vision itself. Sharing with people at all levels is a distinctive feature of vision, for there is no possibility of implementing vision without it. An organization based on sharing will unquestionably be more successful in attaining its vision. Sharing includes identifying others' contributions, co-working with them, and delegating at all levels, convinced that increased growth results from sharing. This includes sharing trust, common values, vision, encouragement, decision-making, and planning. This habit also extends to shared responsibility where authority is not centralized but through subsidiarity and collegiality pushed to the lowest levels in an organization.

Seek integration. There is a great need for integration in our fragmented world. This means seeking depth not superficiality, mutual appreciation not prejudice, connectedness not isolation, self-transcendence not self-centeredness, and team development not hierarchical control. Spiritual leaders value equality, diversity, and social integration. All this requires interpersonal openness, supportive primary groups, and a strong sense of community. This perspective on leadership can only develop when one is free of skepticism, fears, and insecurities regarding one's own and others' roles in the organization. Today, a leader needs to give significance to others, appreciate how much he or she can learn from them, build a sense of friendship, even family, with co-workers, and discover that it can be enjoyable when people, plans, vision, and growth are well integrated.

Stress essentials. A leader who wishes to implement call in a vision must focus on essentials. At a time when many leaders spend so much of their time and a misdirected vision on secondary issues, or even trivia, spiritual leaders must maintain personal and organizational emphases on what is essential to the vision. Of course, what is of primary importance at one time becomes secondary with the passing of time, and a leader constantly evaluates the vision for its authentic focus in changing circumstances. A vision requires adaptation, modification and renewal. Leaders embody flexibility and a readiness to change in order to maintain the relevance and vigor of the vision; stubbornly sticking with non-essentials is not the same as being principled.

Be on the lookout. Leaders seek out, find, and discover whatever can help further the vision of the organization. This will generally be people, often ones who are at the edges or at first seem less likely to contribute. A spiritual leader gives importance to people over laws, emphasizing their dignity, never wanting passivity, and never neglecting to integrate them into the common endeavor. A leader stimulates new ideas and especially the creativity of everyone. One simple test for a leader who is always on the lookout is how he or she treats people who appear as the poorest or least qualified of the group. When a leader is always on the lookout for good ideas, qualified people, new initiatives, fresh articulations of vision, and all forms of creativity, it becomes more likely the vision will endure.

8. Appreciate there is no vision without community.

The call of leadership is a call to be involved in the transformation of the world. In this task each spiritual leader has a unique opportunity and critical responsibility. Leadership implies creating new spaces in which community can be developed, experienced, nourished, tapped for its benefits, and integrated into a vision. First, a leader must build community among all co-workers, and this starts with pleasant and peaceful relationships, discovering participants' gifts that can unify, and encouraging in all followers a spirit of unity, confidence in the importance of community, and a willingness to sacrifice personal desires for the greater good of community. A spiritual leader must know the stages of development of a community, prepare well for group meetings, respectfully summarize group's views, and live in solidarity with all members. A spiritual leader has faith that God's will for human development is to be found in community; community and love together offer the only satisfactory direction for leadership.

Second, a leader is aware that there is a close connection between community and the formation of vision. When there is adequate opportunity for the development of adult relationships in community and the formation of shared values, then the leader can see how components of vision resonate with the community, thus confirming or challenging the values. A leader can reflect on others' contributions, seek consultation, and keep the process open for ongoing input, never closing discussion too soon. Together the members of a community seek truth, share love, and serve the common good, and a leader's tasks include unifying, serving, and building up community in view of its contribution to vision.

Third, a leader appreciates that community has an important role in the ongoing evaluation of vision. This means trusting community, and utilizing the oversight of groups, teams, and the whole community together in the ongoing pursuit of vision. Community can be a teacher, a guru, for so much can be discovered in the honest and qualified assessment of others that can help in the refocusing of vision. For leaders of faith, community is where they can find a sacred presence of God's will, and where they experience the covenantal relationship between God and humanity.

Fourth, a spiritual leader bases decisions for the implementing of vision on the input of community. The arrogant isolation of some leaders and their resistance to community have produced much harm in recent decades. There is a lot of danger of the suppression of vision in privatized leadership. Rather, responding to and learning from community can enrich a leader's approach to vision. Many new values are not so much individual but based on community insights. Nowadays, part of the strategic development of an organization must include the strategic development of a sense of community so that the implementing of vision can be enriched.

9. Develop the building blocks of leadership.

I have mentioned several times that this book's focus is on the personal development of a spiritual leader, and I leave to other books, including my previous two books on leadership, to deal with the nature and development of leadership itself. In this section we look at a series of important building blocks for one's personal response to call and vision.

Be outstanding in managerial skills. Call and vision need the skills of implementation, and a spiritual leader can never afford to be without excellent managerial skills. This will require study, workshops, discussions with peers, web updates, interaction with professional groups, and so on. Leadership skills focus on followers, situations, goals, and personal qualities.

Focus on priorities. A leader needs to deal with personal, organizational, community, and strategic priorities, always maintaining a sense of balance, fairness, and ethics. The key is to give attention to the most important issues in each case, at times even choosing that which is most difficult. Others in the organization can take care of secondary issues, and if the leader deals with the important ones the secondary issues often take care of themselves.

Pursue your own happiness and fulfillment. This is a normal and integral part of vocation. However, happiness and fulfillment are byproducts of one's response to call. Neither is found in immediate satisfaction, pleasure, or gratification, nor even in self-centered achievements. To gain happiness and fulfillment the leader must transcend self and make a positive contribution to other people's lives. Furthermore, a spiritual leader finds happiness and fulfillment in being involved in something for its own sake—goodness, justice, and love.

Put people first. A spiritual leader sets strategies for the development of everyone who works for him or her, both on the level of their competencies and also on the level of their personal development, whether at work, at home, or in the larger community. No one is a means of production, but a subject whose whole person should develop. The more people find growth the more satisfied and fulfilled they will be and the more they will contribute to the organization.

Lead by example. Spiritual leaders must embody the vision and core values of the organization, be people of integrity and credibility whose personal lives should model what they challenge followers to strive for. What a leader says is always secondary to how he or she acts on the issues. Before all else a leader is a model of the vision and values he or she proclaims.

Emphasize communication. A spiritual leader should keep everyone well informed about anything that significantly affects the organization. Most people have no interest to be informed about day to day occurrences; rather daily decisions are best left to managers. Less than twenty percent of organizational issues are significant enough to share with everyone for collaborative input. It is particularly important that leaders inform followers about anything that directly involves them.

Share love and encouragement. A spiritual leader strives every day to show understanding of others, to share ideas and information with them, to give and receive emotional support, to help others and to accept help from them. When people leave the presence of a great leader they know they are loved. Love and encouragement sustain a leader in all his or her efforts. The leader's love and encouragement of followers sustain them too. The leader's love needs to be practical, supplying resources people need, creating a healthy working environment, ensuring security where possible, establishing all the procedures needed in a respectful organization.

Unite mysticism and politics. Mysticism refers to experiences of transcendence, and politics in the broad based sense refers to what happens in society. A spiritual leader can unite these two horizons of life, realizing that one without the other is inadequate. This world's values must be influenced by values beyond this world, and other worldly values become esoteric if they do not impact day to day decisions.

Look to long-term vision. Vision must always lie ahead and as soon as a group begins to achieve the goals of the vision the leader must launch out to new, attractive, demanding, and inspiring goals that are attainable. Generally, the long term is about four to five years, since this is about the equivalent of a generational change.

Set your faith in a personal God. A spiritual leader's life is a manifestation of faith, and he or she takes a stand with this conviction. For the spiritual leader God's presence in our world and in human history is not tentative. God is really present, involved, and interested in all that happens. A leader understands call as coming from God, and vision as the embodiment of God's will for humankind.

10. Make all decisions based on your vision.

A leader needs to make decisions based on the core values, enduring purpose, mission, and vision of the organization. At first this will require a deliberate process until the leader automatically and intuitively responds in light of the vision. He or she will need to maintain calmness, peace, and a reflective mood. Decisions should not merely extend the best of the present into the future, but rather reflect the vision of hope that motivates the leader. Thus, what lies in the future motivates actions in the present. Moreover, since vision is not individualized but rather belongs to the community, decisions based on it should also reflect the will of the community.

Vision is what the organization hopes to do and even become. Frequently, the vision is made more concrete in the organization's mission statement that expresses the key values the community wants to pursue as a faithful expression of their vision. At this point it is useful for the leader and the community to identify the strengths they have that will help them attain the mission and any weaknesses or obstacles that could hinder or block the realization of the group's mission. Since the vision refers to the organization's hopes—four to five years from now—it must be made more immediately accessible in specific goals generally established for each year. Then, even the goals need to be made more concrete in an action plan which is made up of strategies. At this point a leader needs to be precise as to what is to be done, by whom, when, why, and how.

Making decision based on vision seems at first to be a complicated process, but it is not, and one quickly gets used to following these or similar steps to achieve one's goals. Nowadays, it is also very important to evaluate progress in attaining the organization's mission and vision. A leader will ask, how will I know if and when I have been successful? So, he or she will establish specific outcomes to be sought under each strategy. This gives the components of a personal and organizational assessment.

This process of planning, decision-making, and assessment helps a spiritual leader to keep focused on the vision and to see precisely how daily decisions are linked to outcomes, to strategies, to goals, to mission, and then to the attaining of vision.

STEP SIX

LIVE YOUR VISION WITH COURAGE AND PERSEVERANCE

A spiritual leader is a person who brings a different approach to leadership than we have seen in the past. He or she understands the importance of preparing for leadership through a rigorous self training. Such a leader has experienced a change in the direction of life, a conversion that was transformational. This led to awareness of being called to serve others through leadership. The leader then implements the call in a vision that is both personal and organizational. But leadership is an ongoing daily challenge that affects the leader's whole life, and he or she finds that it is imperative to live out the vision with courage and perseverance. In this chapter we look at aspects of the leader's life that enable him or her to continually live the vision of service to which the leader feels called.

1. Institutionalize the vision.

Vision is an expression of a leader's understanding of call, and while it may start with the leader it gradually includes followers' insights and contributions. If this vision is to last in the community served by a spiritual leader, then it needs to be institutionalized. This is a difficult, delicate, and painful task. It is a process of communal commitment to a shared ideal. When a spiritual leader succeeds in institutionalizing the vision, he or she sets in motion an approach that facilitates consensus in selecting, synthesizing, articulating, and evaluating the key components of vision. This enables the community to maintain the vision, renew it as needed, interpret it to ensure ongoing relevance, discover new ways of living it, and generate fresh understandings of it. Institutionalizing vision is part of promoting organizational well-being. A spiritual leader works to make the organization a servant organization, constantly centered on its mission. He or she appreciates the spiritual nature of an organization and upholds for all a compelling vision of what an organization can become. Organizational well-being starts with respect and reverence for each person and with constant effort to create an environment of trust, appreciation, and love, where people are respected for who they are and not just for what they do.

A spiritual leader institutionalizes vision by setting up collegial government for the organization in which participants feel enthused and motivated to live by mission and values. He or she institutionalizes the vision by establishing an administration that is collaborative, uses subsidiarity in decision-making, and fosters and encourages self-managed teams. As the leader stresses self-esteem, compassion, empathy, love, and friendship, he or she builds up the community and its shared vision. To keep the vision alive and relevant a spiritual leader maintains a culture of openness, trust, and ongoing education.

There are four initial components in the institutionalizing of vision. The spiritual leader with followers should develop a values statement, a shared vision, a mission statement, and a strategic plan. Once in place, these can be supported by four useful tools—an executive group, a team charter, a code of ethics, and an oversight board—all dedicated to the core values of the vision. Then, the leader establishes four procedures to support the institutionalizing of vision: hiring procedures, decision-making procedures, conflict management procedures, and due process for the resolution of grievances—all put in place to permeate daily organizational life with the values of the vision.

A spiritual leader understands that an institution is not a dead or static organization but living and growing. It moves through its own growth periods just as an individual does—in fact it has its own psychological stages of development too. So, in institutionalizing a vision one must keep in mind the various stages through which an institution passes, and a spiritual leader will carefully adapt the vision, seeing how it develops paralleling the group's own growth.

2. Awaken others to a new vision.

Part of the spiritual leader's task of institutionalizing the vision is to awaken others to the vision. In this work, the leader's own life and commitment to the values of the vision become a persuasive example and motivator. This work is not easy since a hopeful vision can often look like a frightening risk to others; the challenge of dealing with a new vision, new structures, and new relationships can initially seem threatening. To awaken others to a vision, the spiritual leader will need to be seen as trusting, supporting, and inspiring. Followers will need to find respect for the leader's consistent choices and sense of courage in daring to take risks. The leader must be a person who consistently empowers others, delegates to them, and always celebrates their achievements. Then followers will participate in the vision.

There are a series of practices a spiritual leader can engage in that create an appropriate environment in which to awaken others to a vision. The spiritual leader should control the negative turbulence in the organization. People cannot be empowered when immersed in negativity and low morale. Then, it is important that the leader through hiring practices or training guarantee that teams within the organization share basic values. It is not possible to empower people with whom you do not share basic values; while values do not create vision they do measure the rightness of the chosen direction. The leader needs to share information on important issues and promote open dialogue and questioning, thus fostering multiple perspectives. Key to awakening others to the vision is to establish new structures to release the power of followers—teams, delegations, collaboration. In relation to followers, the leader needs to foster genuine ownership of the vision—perhaps letting them set their own intermediate goals, giving them responsibility. This needs to be followed by ongoing motivation through constant appreciation, encouragement for followers' risk taking, the need for self-evaluation and self-criticism. The spiritual leader should not underestimate stepping aside to let followers feel their own authority for the vision. In one way or another, the spiritual leader must encourage the enthusiasm and passion of followers, and make them aware that the vision is theirs to enhance. When followers feel appreciated in their work and supported in their dreams, they are more likely to feel awakened to the shared vision. However, a leader should be aware that most people never identify a hundred percent with a vision. Each one is partially identified. The leader strives to awaken people more fully to the shared vision while appreciating it will never be total—that is what keeps the vision open to change.

3. Keep a hold on the vision.

An important task for a leader is to hold on to the vision. A leader can delegate a lot, but must retain a sense of responsibility for the personal and organizational vision. This means a careful management of the vision, and while a leader can always be willing to compromise on secondary issues, he or she must be scrupulous in maintaining the core values of the vision. However, even on this issue a leader should not arrogantly think that only he or she understands the primary components of vision. Most leaders fail when it comes to implementing the vision. There are two situations that can lead to the insidious destruction of a vision. The leader can forget about the foundational values of the vision in his or her rush to adapt and implement it in changing circumstances. Or, he or she so clings to former expressions that the vision loses its relevance. A leader requires balance, and must be ever faithful to the vision and yet bold enough to search for new ways of expressing its relevance. In a previous section I mentioned three key words that guide fidelity to vision: root, interpret, and discover. Everything a leader does must be rooted in the original vision, but he or she needs to avoid fundamentalism regarding the vision. Expressions of vision change in order to maintain relevance, but cannot be spontaneous expressions unrelated to the original common shared vision. So, leaders must step up and preside over the vision, but must also be ready to change those aspects that are not essential in order to preserve the core values. In this responsibility they can capitalize on the gifts of other dedicated members of the organization.

The vision is primarily one of hope; a God-given vision for humanity as applied to the leader's own organization. So, the leader in holding on to the vision and persevering in its values should retain a real sense of the Gospel's challenges to a hope-filled vision. The Bible is first of all a source of inspiration and edification. The leader should have a sense of Scripture's priorities and a feel for what disciples of another age felt; as long as we remember that their situations are not ours. A leader discovers a mentality and perspective which he or she can then live out in new situations, unforeseen by the Bible. Scripture is a source, an inspired synthesis, a vision of what discipleship was understood to be two thousand years ago. It is a point of departure, a useful measuring rod, and a leader can dialogue with its challenges and listen to its call to action. Each leader must now reinterpret it, reformulate its call, and live out its challenges in new ways, more relevant to our own times. To do this appropriately, leader and followers alike need a firm commitment to ethical values, ongoing education, and courageous perseverance to make their organization into a servant organization.

4. Embody the vision in a spirituality.

Vision and spirituality are two aspects of a person's or an organization's life; two ways of looking at the future we strive to make real, at the call we hear and are restless to achieve, and at the hopes that draw us forward. One without the other gives a program of action unconnected with one's inner self, or spiritual values unconnected with daily life. Only when these two aspects of life and leadership are integrated does the leader find fulfillment. Leadership is both the inward journey into the core of a person's spirit and an external journey expressing those hoped-for values in an action plan of vision. The former is who you are as a leader, and the latter is what you hope to become and to do because of who you are. It is unacceptable to have a spirituality that is merely believed-in and has no impact on the here and now. It is also unacceptable to have a vision for the here and now without being influenced by values of the inner spirit. Leadership today is spiritual leadership.

Spirituality is important in living the vision for several reasons. It gives us insight into the meaning of life, provides an understanding of right and wrong, and gives us a sense of belonging to community. It also generates a sense of mystery, awe, and excitement; a feeling of security and peace; and an understanding that decisions in this life should be made in light of an afterlife. Spirituality means striving to become one's best self. It embraces all of life, making sure every aspect of life reflects higher values. All these components of spirituality are also components of leadership, especially when focused on vision. Spirituality is about developing relationships—with oneself, with other people, with communities and organizations, with the world around us, and with God. Spirituality impacts daily life with the best values of humanity through decisions and actions based on motivating values. Spirituality is not only what we do but what God does in and through us, drawing us to a better life and transforming the world through our efforts.

A leader's appealing vision today includes the values of the spirit, the challenge of how our work ought to be done, the emphasis on the importance of faith, hope, and love, and the experience of transformational presence. A spiritual leader permeates his or her endeavors to live out the vision with the spirit of the beatitudes. Vision today is an expression of one's inner spirit and soul; it is an immersion in what humanity can become; it includes a desire to live with mystery and to pursue it with passion. In the formulation of vision, leadership explores the best of who we are called to be and achieves the best of which we are capable. Nowadays, there is no genuine leadership or vision without spirituality, without the inner greatness of spirit and soul that transforms one's leadership. If a leader is to live the vision with courage and perseverance, it will be because he or she is motivated by a profound spirituality.

5. Remember your prophetical calling.

Vision determines what needs to be done in the present because of how the leader sees the future. That is exactly what a prophet does—he tells the community how they ought to live in the present because of what he sees as God's desired future for the community. A prophet speaks out of conviction, and his work has three different focuses in three different periods of history— remove injustice, console and support in hard times, and encourage others to look forward with hope. These tasks are not unlike a leader's in challenging followers to maintain the vision; his or her role is to be a counter-pull to contemporary warped values in leadership.

Contemporary spiritual leadership has a prophetical component to it. Spiritual leaders are called and set apart. The leader's life, like the prophet's, will never be easy and each one will need strength of character to persevere in the task. The prophet's message is not always acceptable, and a prophetical leader will often be marginalized. Prophetical leaders move people beyond the present, drawn by the challenge of the vision. The prophetical leader implements the vision in practical involvement; he or she exercises a leadership that is proactive, always in favor of vision. A prophetical leader must always expect significant rejection; in fact the more a prophetical leader insists on the values of the vision, the more some people turn away. A spiritual leader needs resilience. Nevertheless, he or she must make every effort to seek responsiveness in followers, so that the vision can be shared.

A contemporary leader who wishes to live the vision with courage and perseverance will need to be a prophet. A prophet knows his or her whole life is given over to proclaiming a vision. Such a leader will do anything and everything to bring the vision to reality, carrying out the mission with both patience and urgency. Above all the prophet must be authentic, knowing that leadership is not about improving one's own status, but about interpreting and implementing a vision. For such a leader everything he or she does must reflect the vision. Like the prophets of old, a contemporary prophetical leader must confront injustice, denounce half-heartedness, and remind people of their obligations to the vision. He or she must give consolation and encouragement in times of trial and hardship. Then, the leader encourages and fills others with hope as they dedicate themselves to rebuild, refocus, and re-energize the vision.

A prophetical spiritual leader has spiritual perception and sees things within the consciousness and awareness of God's vision. He or she raises the moral standard of an organization, reminds participants of the need for obedience to the vision of God, and makes people aware of God's judgment of humanity. The prophetical leader often finds that what is clear to him or her is unintelligible to some followers. In this case, the intensity of the leader's convictions regarding vision become the source of persuasion for others.

Prophetical leaders are creative, as they challenge people to reshape the future of organizations in spite of the lurking danger from people who want to preserve the status quo. This can be a dangerous undertaking, for the selfishly powerful do not like to change what they can use to their own advantage. As the prophetical leader looks to the vision, he or she challenges people to believe things can and must be different. This means dismantling dominant structures, providing alternative ways for people to live in society, and introducing new relationships in communities. The need for leaders to take a prophetical stance on all aspects of ethics today is desperately needed in all kinds of organizational life. This kind of leadership is revolutionary, as it uproots structures of leadership based on power and replaces them with service. Leadership is a form of prophecy.

6. Emphasize the transcendent.

I have insisted since the beginning of the book that leadership results from a profound spiritual experience—a conversion and a call. Many leaders now are everyday mystics—they appreciate the transcendent in leadership. They know intangibles are as important as tangibles. If the prophet is one who has understood the hoped-for vision in the revelations of Scripture, the mystical leader is one who has experienced the vision in an encounter with the realm of the Spirit. Such a leader is a person of interiority and hope and builds the vision on what he or she has experienced of respect, justice, compassion, community, mutuality, and love. In times of prayerful reflection, such a leader encounters the call of the living God, challenging him or her to be faithful to a new vision. This is not a vague or esoteric experience; rather it is a very concrete vision of how to treat other people in organizations. It is not a managerial plan of action, but a vision of just and true human interactions. Of course, mystical leaders who appreciate the transcendent aspects of life must be competent and get the job done, but they have experienced a vision that draws and inspires them.

A spiritual leader, open to the transcendent, finds a new way of being a leader. In contemplative reflection, he or she discovers God's vision of how a leader serves humanity. The leader appreciates his or her role in the world, receives a sense of peace and calmness, and is centered and inner directed. Certainly, the spiritual leader realizes at depth that leadership is a personal vocation, and this awareness leads to a new way of interacting with others. More than anything else a person who places self in a deeper relationship with God discovers that God's relationship with humanity is essentially one of love, and such a leader understands that God now acts, hopes, loves, and serves through him or her. This moves the leader to live and work for the building up of community whether within the organization or in outreach to other groups. Experiencing the presence of God gives one a more objective understanding of the world with its goodness and its evil. With this awareness comes the challenge to struggle for change that reveals a vision of hope and love. A genuine experience of God in contemplative reflection is immediate and intuitive. The picture of oneself and one's call to leadership is clear and allows no discussion. A leader who is open to the transcendent knows immediately what he or she has to do to be faithful to the vision.

A spiritual leader sees the extraordinary in the midst of our ordinary lives and approaches this world's problems with the values of God. In doing so, he or she tries to change the world and make sure that the world does not change his or her values. The life of a leader who is close to God enables him or her to stay rooted; he or she gains insight from the experience, listens attentively, constantly seeking guidance, and always ready to take a stand for the vision of the future. This exercise of leadership is of its nature dynamic, not fundamentalist. Such a person is a contemplative leader, a voice of God reminding followers of the vision for which they must relentlessly strive.

7. Focus on your charisms and the community's charisms.

Spiritual leaders are specially gifted people, and they recognize that their gifts are from God; we call such gifts charisms and such individuals are charismatic leaders. The prophetical leader emphasizes what the community ought to be. The mystical leader experiences the values of the vision. The charismatic leader has the gifts that create the vision. He or she is endowed with special gifts for the up-building of community and the implementing of vision. This awareness of special gifts of leadership needs to be linked to humility, so one does not exaggerate one's own importance. It also needs awareness that others are also gifted. An authentic charismatic leader always realizes he or she works with a charismatic community. It is this mutual appreciation of each other's gifts that enriches community and facilitates the implementing of vision. Genuine charismatic leaders are humble and treat others with graciousness; pseudo-charismatics are arrogant and autocratically impose their worldview on others. Spiritual leaders appreciate their gifts have a social function—they are for the benefit of the community. However, charismatic leadership is not enough; it must be complemented with the daily transformational skills of good management-leadership.

Charisms are gifts, but a spiritual leader can prepare for these gifts by cultivating values of the spirit and by an openness of heart, receptivity, and a constant sense of gratitude. Such a leader not only leads well but also lives well, giving example of the values that implement the vision. Leaders need to be great listeners, and a charismatic leader listens for the gentle reminders of the Spirit, urging on the challenge of the vision. He or she can hear needs in people's non-verbal responses as well as in their words, in the signs of the times, in the cries of the needy, and in the hopes of society—all challenging regarding vision. A charismatic leader appreciates the best of himself or herself comes from gifts, and this makes the leader aware of the need to be open and receptive to what life brings, and to be watchful for all the gifts that others have received for building up the community. This moves the leader to a profound sense of gratitude to God for his or her own gifts and for all the gifts within the community. This kind of leader knows that a shared commitment to the vision requires that he or she release the gifts of others and channel their energy, talents, and hopes to implement it. Such leaders live immersed in the presence of goodness, experience a sense of humility before the wonders of life, and cherish other people and their gifts. Perhaps more than anything else a spiritual leader realizes that he or she is a gift for others in his or her leadership, and needs to give others the opportunity to use their gifts too. One of the temptations of a charismatic leader is to interpret other people's gifts in light of his or her own. A spiritual leader should not domesticate other's gifts but leave them in their own originality to challenge, refocus, and correct the shared vision.

8. Remember your role as a healer.

There is an intimate link between leadership and healing. A spiritual leader focuses on integrated, holistic approaches to people and to organizations, removing what is sick and dysfunctional, bringing harmony, striving for wellness, and thus enriching the vision. We have already seen how a leader repairs the harm of the past, but anything that negatively affects the well-being of individuals and organizations needs healing—and this is an ongoing responsibility. The leader is constantly striving to transform minds and hearts so that all can give themselves healthily to living the vision with courage and perseverance. The first focus of a leader's healing is his or her own failures in life and in leadership. This is part of the leader's own ongoing conversion. The leader also sees need for healing others—those in pain for one reason or another; those who are stunted in their personal fulfillment; those hurt by former leaders' incompetence and insensitivity; those who have been or are the objects of prejudice in any of its forms. Furthermore, spiritual leaders are aware that organizations are often sick and dysfunctional, have harmful environments and structures, and become oppressive and destructive. There are many casualties of sick organizations that are filled with disharmony and lack of balance. All this needs healing too.

Spiritual leaders in their striving to implement a vision become aware of their need to heal. They should review their organization and discern what needs healing. This diagnostic phase names what needs to change and challenges the community to become involved in the transformative healing. A spiritual leader will use whatever skills seem best to achieve healing—therapeutic, psychological, educational, spiritual, and community skills. Old approaches to leadership implied power, control, dominance, but spiritual leaders are forgiving, healing, loving, and enabling.

An important component of a leader's responsibility in encouraging all to live the vision with courage and perseverance is to cultivate a spirit of reconciliation in the whole community. While reconciliation is unquestionably one of the most important characteristics of Christianity—St. Paul equates it with salvation, the reality is that we fail so much in living it. In fact, we seem more often to be communities and organizations immersed in divisiveness rather than reconciliation and unity. Reconciliation needs honesty, faith, reflection, and a common desire to live the vision. It implies total self-gift to others and complete acceptance of others. It is a task of mutual forgiveness. The spiritual leader constructs a reconciling community by fostering mutual acceptance, especially in diverse groups, by building bridges between people of different religious, social, economic, and political backgrounds, and by insisting on respect for everyone's opinion.

A further dimension of a healing leader's responsibility is building an environment of mutual compassion. Compassion means to share someone's pain, to understand their fears and anxieties, and to remember their humanity and desire for healing. It means feeling the way others do in pain, being present to them and enduring pain with them, and supporting them through their trials. It also means not sitting by in comfort while others suffer, not allowing an organization to wallow in mutual blame. It means candor, honesty, truth-telling, facing the hard realities of life together, and working to remove the pain that it is possible to remove. Spiritual leaders live the vision with courage and perseverance as they strive to bring healing to their organization and its people.

9. Pay the price of maintaining the vision.

A leader oversees the mission, values, and vision of an organization within the larger vision of hope for humanity. He or she not only works at this, but it becomes an intimate part of life. This personal journey of a spiritual leader is a very hard and demanding pilgrimage which I believe has two stages to it. The first stage is an active one in which the leader does all that is possible to achieve goals and mission. It is filled with activities, as the leader feels everything depends on him or her; it is a leadership of tasks, skills, goals, plans, strategies, evaluations, and so on. The second stage in leadership is more passive, reflective, contemplative, and receptive. While stage one stresses doing, stage two stresses being—the leader realizes that everything does not depend on him or her. So, the second stage focuses more on imagination, contemplation, community skills, values, and vision. Stage two still needs all the skills of stage one, but transforms those skills with a new awareness that comes with the spiritual experience of stage two. Most leaders stay in stage one, and they are very good. Those who journey to stage two bring a new meaning to work, to relationships, to ethics and justice, and to institutional purpose, mission, and vision.

The transition from stage one to stage two is painful for a leader—the price he or she must pay to be faithful to vision. The leader experiences a crisis regarding what he or she has been doing as a leader and feels leadership has to change. The leader transitions from an old way of viewing leadership to a new one, feeling there is more to life and leadership than first thought. But, letting go, leaving behind, abandoning what was thought to be good, are all part of a painful refocusing of life and leadership. There follows a sense of shock, discouragement, a feeling of previous failure, fear at the unknown that lies ahead, and emptiness as one leaves behind former success, competence, skills, and vision. However, the leader must step out beyond the former comfort zone, let go of the past, and open one's mind and heart to a new way of being a leader, being a spiritual leader. This is an experience of illumination in which the leader receives a call to the renewal of leadership.

In stage one the leader feels in control, emphasizes personal strengths, knowledge, and leadership, and finds everything centered on the leader. Then, he or she loses all this security and feels lost and insecure. Ahead he or she discovers a vision of faith and hope, appreciates quiet time and reflection, senses that a new power from a realm beyond the ordinary is now in control, and knows he or she has been called to serve as a leader and to be a worthy channel of a vision centered on transcendent values. The journey of a leader is painful, but we need men and women who are willing to endure the hardship of transition and thus become qualitatively different kinds of leaders.

10. Celebrate the vision.

To persevere in fidelity to a vision needs the commitment of everyone in the community. Therefore, a leader must keep all members focused on the vision. This starts with hiring procedures that give a leader opportunity to show how proud he or she is about the vision. New hires should see the leader celebrating the shared vision of the group. This pride in the vision continues with the leader taking whatever occasions present themselves to teach the members of the organization about the vision. There will be plenty of times to facilitate the shared input of the group, but a leader appreciates teaching about values, mission, and vision is a critical part of his or her responsibility. Some organizations post key concepts of vision around the working environment, and this too becomes a celebration of the group's shared identity, as well as contributing to reminding and teaching the followers about their shared values.

A leader can also celebrate his or her own successes regarding the vision. He or she should be proud at achievements and celebrate them. After all, the leader must maintain his or her own motivation and ongoing dedication. Part of a leader's own motivation is giving time to thinking about the vision, studying the key ideas, and praying for success. In times of quiet contemplative reflection a leader celebrates the vision in his or her own heart.

Equally important to the above is celebrating the vision with the whole organization. There are occasions each year—anniversaries, founder's days, end or year reports, and so on—when the leader can bring the group together in a non-disruptive way to celebrate the whole group's commitment and their common achievements. Such occasions are always opportunities for the leader to focus attention, teach, and celebrate.

An important contribution to prolonging vision is to celebrate personal contributions to it. Honoring significant achievements with public recognition gives the leader the opportunity to reinforce values, to teach, and to motivate. While celebrating a person's reaching a goal is important, such celebrations also motivate others to strive for excellence that will be recognized. Giving importance to people and their contributions reinforces values, encourages discretionary commitment, shows people how much they are appreciated, and gives further focus to vision. Public recognition and celebration must never be perfunctory. Celebrating is a precise leadership skill. It needs little time to be effective, but it must be authentic from the leader and special to the recipient. If rewards accompany celebration, they do not need to be financial. In fact, most genuine celebrations cost nothing. Not all celebrations need to be public, although being so gives the leader occasion to refocus attention on vision and teach and clarify the organization's values. A sensitive leader will keep himself or herself well informed about workers' efforts and successes, so that when opportunities present themselves the leader can encounter an individual, express awareness of achievement, thank the person, and give the special recognition that is deserved. Stopping someone in the factory or office and celebrating achievement is particularly appreciated when it is spontaneous. A worker then knows that a leader's staff did not give the information or arrange the celebration, but the leader personally took notice and was directly involved. As a spiritual leader, be proud of your people, know and appreciate their work, celebrate their successes. All this reinforces your dedication to the shared vision of the organization.

STEP SEVEN

ESTABLISH SUPPORTS FOR YOUR SPIRITUAL LEADERSHIP

If you feel called to be a spiritual leader, to dedicate your whole life in the service of others, then you will need to be prudent enough to arrange for yourself a series of strong supports that can help maintain your dedication. At first, all these take time and explicit decisions, but as time goes on they become a normal part of your life, and you would not want to be without them. These supports enrich your leadership but also every aspect of your life, helping you become a better person, spouse, friend, parent, and member of community. Leadership describes something about how you wish to live, the kind of person you want to be. Make sure you support your commitment carefully.

1. Develop strategies against excessive stress.

The profound and rapid changes in modern life challenge leaders to constantly change and be creative in responding to the complexities of life. Leaders often find that followers' unwillingness to change or the fact that they have a different value system can be stressful. If leaders are tempted to set unrealistic goals for themselves or develop a perfectionist tendency, then stress results. Leadership challenges are often intensified by constant need to meet deadlines, by lack of financial resources, and by changes that demand new skills from the leader.

When the stresses of life become so great that a leader can no longer cope with them, they lead to distress. When the stresses result from pressures of interaction with people, they can lead to the possible development of burnout. This phenomenon does not necessarily result from overwork. In fact, the workaholic is not a candidate for burnout, since he or she uses work as an escape from people. It is when people in certain professions, like spiritual leaders, find themselves immersed in people problems that burnout begins. It develops in three stages. First, leaders become dissatisfied at work, feel a lack of appreciation from others, and begin to isolate themselves. This stage does not affect the quality of work and leadership, and others often do not even notice it, since the symptoms are no different than other temporary stressful situations. Second, a time of self-questioning leads to a feeling of helplessness and frustration. This can become so great that job performance and leadership begin to suffer. Third, terminal burnout is present when leaders begin to mechanically perform their tasks without any real interest or quality involvement. At this stage, leaders feel intense loneliness, can become sour on life, and often manifest an open rebellion that completely disrupts their leadership. This last stage ends with individuals hating the very situation that they believe causes the stress, their own vocation in leadership.

The symptoms of burnout are similar to those of general stress: headaches, insomnia, loss of appetite, irritability, fatigue, chest pains, and lack of energy. A leader with burnout loses desire to go to his or her place of work or to associate with followers. Such a potential burnout victim becomes constantly discouraged, angry, and overly sensitive to other people's remarks. At first, the natural tendency is to increase one's commitment at work to prove to oneself and others that there is really no problem. Once the burnout cycle begins it is very difficult to stop it, so prevention is critical, so that quality leaders do not suffer in this way.

Among the practices that a leader can develop to insure a lifestyle that avoids burnout are the following. Leaders should admit the seriousness of stress in leadership, then give adequate time to reflection, friendship, leisure, and broad interests outside of one's working environment. A leader should provide himself or herself with suitable educational opportunities to keep one's mind alert and appreciate the depths and limits of leadership as a call to be, more than to do. Make sure you have a support system that constantly gives you encouragement and feedback. Improve the quality of your working environment. Redefine success in leadership so as to benefit from job satisfaction. Maintain deep relationships that provide intimacy and love. Take care of yourself physically with proper nutrition, regular exercise, and sufficient sleep. It is important that leaders take care to prevent burnout. After all, burnout only affects the very best.

2. Align your leadership with your values.

A major support for your spiritual leadership is the personal integrity that you have fostered and that others have seen in you over the years. People need to know that your core values guide your decision-making and that your judgments reflect character. This implies that as a leader you constantly form your conscience, that part of your inner spirit that evaluates right and wrong. Your decisions as a leader must portray your self-concept, which is invested with values to which you must be faithful. If you do not change what you oppose you legitimize it, and it becomes a part of you. Your decisions manifest your understanding of the human person, that you believe the dignity of human beings takes precedence over all else, and that all you do must be at the service of human development and the common good. You must never stifle conscience, but respond to the challenges of your inner self.

Supporting your spiritual leadership through ongoing conscience formation means constant self-evaluation—checking how you reacted to ethical deliberations in the past. It requires reflection on how you approached decisions, what role prudence played, and the input and evaluation of significant others—whether teachers, thinkers, or doers. Change is rapid, personal decisions risky, and so one always needs humility when others may correctly judge decisions to be outside shared values. Then the leader must refocus and go on, without discouragement to make other decisions, for not to decide is also a decision. Ongoing conscience formation is part of the support for one's spiritual leadership. Leaders who are dedicated to aligning with values know they need high accountability, and always show responsibility to others both above and below them in the organization. Such a leader puts others first, knows authority is at the service of others, and creates an environment that reflects values. Followers recognize a man or woman who aligns leadership with values by honesty, truthfulness, nurturing relationships, and universal respect.

Maintaining a commitment to values in your leadership requires reflection, meditation, and prayer. Many management books suggest a short quiet time at the beginning of the day helps in prioritizing the day's agenda. However, it is far more important that a leader have times to reflectively assess whether what he or she plans to do fits in with stated values. Many organizations have office retreats that focus on all kinds of issues. There should also be times of quiet reflective withdrawal to see that work and organizations are aligned with values.

From time to time leaders find they align themselves with false or useless values; things that are done because they have always been done; organizational values that died years ago but are kept on life-support; policies, practices, and procedures that are in place because some former leader picked up the idea in a workshop. A spiritual leader must systematically examine the culture and practices of both himself or herself and the organization, and get rid of what everyone knows is useless. This too is part of the support needed to focus with clarity on one's leadership.

3. Create space for yourself.

Spiritual leaders support their commitment by creating space for themselves. They need space and distance from daily involvement, time to think, be quiet, reflect, and rekindle dedication to their calling. They should always guarantee themselves freedom to be alone, cultivating a solitude that refreshes. Each leader should discover a time and place that creates distance from work and offers opportunity to be alone in the presence of God. This time is a leader's sacred time or *kairos*, and this space is sacred space, one's own desert encounter. When leaders so often suffer from stimulus overload, creating this kind of space is an urgent need. This should be a change in the use of time and of space that leads to forgetfulness of self, and an immersion in interior peace.

This special space and time is more than leisure, it is sacred space. It is an opportunity to live in one's own time free of pressures and also an opportunity to live in God's time. During these occasions, a leader can wait in stillness, listen in silence, and open self to the guidance of the Spirit. This sacred space offers challenges of awakening and enlightenment, as the leader listens to the call and directions of the Spirit. This special space and time provide the peace and tranquility needed to think about one's commitment, to bring perspective to one's role as a leader, to immerse oneself in the call and challenges of God. It also produces clarity of vocation, renewal of dedication, and a reinvigoration and re-energizing of one's personal leadership.

A spiritual leader learns to enjoy this time and space and becomes attentive to the passivity, realizing things happen in this space and time that do not happen elsewhere or at other times. Such a leader finds the experience is filled with wonder, mystery, and admiration, and he or she approaches the experience with reverence. When a leader takes time to withdraw in quiet and reflective space, he or she learns to see the extraordinary in the ordinary. Although this is a very simple, quiet period of withdrawal, it can be an intense time when the leader can unravel the complexities of life and see things as they are. This is a time to see connections and to appreciate the extraordinary presence of God in the normal events of each day. I have mentioned already in passing the gift of a spiritual leader to live here in this world while always being elsewhere—in the presence of reality beyond the normal events of each day. When a leader can cultivate this dual presence of the here-and-now and the there-and-then, he or she can make decisions permeated with spiritual values. A spiritual leader who creates space for himself or herself away from the clutter of daily life will nourish spiritual leadership.

4. Find a supportive community.

One of the delightful supports of one's spiritual leadership is to be surrounded by a supportive community. A leader immersed in daily responsibilities can often experience loneliness, hurt, and rejection. It is painful to be surrounded by people who cannot hope or be enthused about anything, or by others who seem to live calmly with diminished notions of love, justice, community, and human fulfillment. A leader must often work with sick people or with healthy people who have sick attitudes. Some organizations even evidence a tribal ferocity to each other or to other groups. The leader can often feel marginalized in his or her own organization. Finding a supportive community can give a leader a chance for healing, recuperation, and emotional support, even when the leader does not even realize he or she needs it.

When a leader has a supportive community made up of people the leader is glad to be with, it can have an enriching and strengthening effect on leadership. When a leader surrounds himself or herself with like-minded people, it can be a refreshing and healthy experience. When people love each other and are there for each other, it leads to a sense of release, harmony, and togetherness. This community can be at different levels; peers, groups, family, mentors, and some close intimate friends. Together they can develop a vision of a loving, supportive community. If the members develop their community, it can become caring, respectful of each other, and dedicated to a shared vision. Such a group sustains the leader when he or she is weary, and it becomes a standard of shared values that can be threatened in daily life. Likewise, the community can call the leader's attention to issues, remind him or her of vocational responsibilities, and summon the best that the leader aspires to. Generally, the leader finds comfort in the group, knows the community's love is unquestioned, and can be free to be himself or herself.

A leader sets aside time to be with a supportive community. While he or she spends most of professional life with groups, he or she is generally the animator and the support of others. However, a leader needs a group where he or she is nurtured and supported. It ought to be a group that understands the leader's values and vision, shares them, and sustains the commitment. This is not just a friendship group, nor simply a peer professional group. Rather, the supportive community a leader needs must be at a similar level of commitment as the leader and shares at the level of knowledge, values, emotion, and dedication. It can be a group of peers or a spontaneously formed group, but it matures with supports of friendship and common responsibilities. In such a community a leader can be at rest, refocus, and renew himself or herself.

5. Seek enlightenment from a strong personal faith.

In a spiritual leader's life there are times and experiences that are very special. These transforming experiences give insight into the meaning of one's life as a leader. The experience is the basis of faith—we discover and then believe that we are called, loved, gifted, and missioned to serve others in leadership. We do not study this; it is the result of an experience of God in our lives. It may well express itself in a belief system, but the experience itself is what remains with us, challenging and motivating us in our commitment to spiritual leadership. The initial experience may arise from some simple event, but we feel immersed in a sense of wonder and awe, and we know we have touched a reality beyond the ordinary. We recognize what has happened as a gift of God and receive it with gratitude. This faith-filled experience teaches us about values that should inspire our lives; it becomes a guide to how we ought to live; it is an experience of enlightenment regarding our vocation to leadership. Generally, this experience in which we place our faith is an experience of God's love for us and for humanity, and at the same time it is an appreciation that we have an important role in this life that we never glimpsed before.

A spiritual leader bases his or her life on the personal transforming experience of faith in God's call. This leads to two movements: one is a movement away from former understandings of God, oneself and one's role in the world, others and their place in contemporary life. At the same time it is a movement towards a new understanding of God, of oneself and one's role, of others and their importance to God, and of the world as a gift for the common good. The personal faith becomes an experience of enlightenment regarding one's leadership; how to live the kind of leadership God wants of visionary spiritual people.

This experience of enlightenment is an encounter with God that one will never forget. It might be simple, will rarely be filled with signs and wonders, but the spiritual leader knows he or she has touched a different level of reality and will never be the same again. Generally one can remember when this happened, where one was, what the experience was all about, and what were the core values seen in the experience. Following this encounter a spiritual leader commits himself or herself to re-live the core values in leadership, feels accountable for the experience, and has a sense of responsibility to be faithful to the core values of the experience.

Now and again as a spiritual leader you should pause in the midst of your many responsibilities and reflect on a particular peak experience that was special to you. Describe how you felt following this experience. Ask yourself if this was a moment of enlightenment. What is different about your understanding of God, yourself, others, your leadership after the experience than what you understood before? Identify the key core values you learned in the experience. Savor and express gratitude for the encounter you had in faith. Reflect on how you must live differently because of the experience you had. As you seek enlightenment from this strong personal faith, let it permeate all you do in leadership.

6. Become a contemplative leader.

Leaders need to be reflective people, but more than that they need to be contemplative. Reflection is the laborious, intellectual meditation—thinking things through, reasoning, applying insights, drawing conclusions. Contemplation is intuitive, immediate, passive perception of reality. It is not only cognitive but emotional—it is a form of immediate knowledge permeated by love. It is a gift that often comes to people who prepare well for it. Such people treasure honest self-knowledge, solitude, freedom and detachment, and they appreciate beauty, joy, and enthusiasm. They practice self-control, choose suitable times and places conducive to reflection, look after their bodily health, and nourish their spirit with good, sound, spiritually enriching reading and reflection.

When a leader becomes contemplative there follows a series of effects that transform his or her personal life and leadership. Such a leader discovers peace, harmony, self-contentment, and an increased commitment to morality. A contemplative leader receives enlightenment, an expansion of consciousness, and an awakening to the richness of life. There follows forgetfulness of self, a desire to do God's will, a passion for service, interior peace, spiritual energy, and compassion towards others. Contemplation is a gift of God received passively by a spiritual leader, and it transforms his or her life and leadership—the way of seeing self, of working with others, of building local community, and of serving the human community.

The leader who supports his or her dedication with contemplation can analyze issues more immediately and with greater clarity, can respond to demands more directly, and can appreciate people's interactions more perceptively. More than anything else a contemplative person perceives immediately— there is no time in life when one sees more clearly than when one is in union with God in contemplative prayer. At that time, no one can argue, delay, find excuses, or modify demands. Rather, one sees oneself before God as one is in perfect clarity—who one is, who one is called to be, and how one must respond,

So, one of the great supports of your spiritual leadership is contemplation. In this experience your reflection and your leadership come together. To be part of this process you need to feel comfortable with yourself, not be afraid to be alone, and have a well-focused sense of purpose. You must appreciate the call of a realm of life beyond this one and create for yourself opportunities to reflect, and establish adequate open-ended time for prayer. You must learn to listen, to be inspired, to concentrate, and to live peacefully in silent receptivity. In the past, we often valued leaders who were doers and achievers. Today we need reflective thinkers who can bring forth new insights as a result of the peace, concentration, and perception that come with contemplation. It is one of the best supports of a spiritual leader.

7. Accept the power that is offered you.

There are three fundamental energies of the human spirit that provide a special form of power to the person who appreciates them. These three dynamic qualities are faith, hope, and love. They do not refer to attitudes that we might evidence—having faith in someone, finding hope in a future project, showing love to those in need. Such would be moral virtues that people can manifest in their daily dealings with others. These three fundamental energies of the soul are gifts of God that transform one's personality—they are known as theological virtues to distinguish them from simple human acts and attitudes. They are gifts of God that change the way we deal with life.

A spiritual leader gets to know more and more about life and people by the constant accumulation of knowledge. This is the work of one's intellect. However, it is possible to know more about life, human purpose, and development by stopping the accumulation of information and focusing beyond the intellect to faith. What a spiritual leader believes about people, humanity's destiny, God's will, is far greater than what he or she can learn from accumulated information. This faith is a revelation of life, community, and human purpose. Likewise, a spiritual leader gains so much from the accumulation of good memories—one's own, communities', human history's. He or she can remember the best that good people have achieved. However, if the leader stops remembering and instead allows himself or herself to focus on the God-given future, the leader will find far greater challenges in hope than in the accumulation of memories. This hope is a gift of God that sets the direction for one's life and leadership. It is also possible for a spiritual leader to gain insight into human need and development by focusing on what men and women want in their daily lives. They have many wants, desires, aspirations, and presumed needs, and a leader can see common trends in the accumulation of human desires. If, instead of focusing on the objects of the will, the spiritual leader stops this emphasis and stresses the one great yearning of human beings that satisfies all their searching, he or she will see the transformative impact of love. Thus, one's intellect is transformed by faith, one's memories by hope, and one's desires by love. These three theological virtues are the greatest supports for a spiritual leader whose life then centers on faith, hope and love in all he or she does. This is the most practical plan of action for a leader. Everything else is partial and temporary—it cannot be ignored in daily dealings, but a vision that comes from faith, hope, and love is what channels a person's spiritual leadership. You will need knowledge as long as you know true vision comes from faith—what you believe motivates you. You will gain so much from remembering the best that leaders can do, as long as you know memories are never as powerful as hope.

As a leader you must be attentive to people's desires, and yet must always be aware that it is love alone that satisfies their restless spirits.

8. Be aware of stages in your growth as a leader.

We are accustomed to developmental stages in life, in spiritual development, in group growth, and so on. There are also development stages in leadership. In fact, for a spiritual leader his or her human, spiritual, and leadership development form parts of one integrated self-understanding—all three wax or wane together. The spiritual leader's life is a struggle to become his or her best self by transcending self-centeredness and developing enriching relationships with others and with God. It is a movement towards fullness of life, the best actualization of one's humanity, through cooperation and responsibility and the powerful action of God's grace.

It is possible to view leadership development in four simple stages, four emphases that are gradually integrated. The first stage is when a person focuses exclusively on the task at hand and uses instrumental skills to achieve the goals. The leader tends to stress his or her own abilities. The second stage continues to emphasize the importance of task and instrumental skills but adds the importance of relationship-building and interpersonal skills. Along with this goes the emphasis on participatory leadership when the leader works with others to achieve the goals of the common endeavor. The third stage incorporates the first two—task and relationships, instrumental and interpersonal skills, but moves to include the creativity that comes from interiority. The leader now assumes his or her own authority, prominence, and stature, and finds strength from values within his or her inner spirit. At this time the leader appreciates the values of collegiality and begins to stress the specifically Christian aspects of leadership. This is part of an integrated vision of leadership. The fourth stage develops from stage three and includes and integrates the previous three emphases on task, relationships, and interiority, but now moves to a vision of community where the leader sees everything he or she does in relation to the common good and the genuine aspirations of everyone in the community. The leader now values the qualities of the heart and the transforming values of love as part of building a caring community. This is when the leader fosters his or her prophetical, mystical, charismatic, and healing dimensions of leadership.

Many leaders go no further than stage two, but as a spiritual leader you must move ahead, for only in the later stages does one evidence the specifically Christian values of leadership. From the kind of leadership you live, others can readily identify what you believe about your own role and mission, about other people and their hopes and dreams, and about your relationship to God. If you keep these stages before your mind, the vision of what lies ahead in leadership can constantly motivate you as you strive to become who you are capable of being. Leadership is always a combination of vision and skills. You must see to it that you develop the skills of each stage—task oriented skills, interpersonal skills, skills that come from reflection, interiority, and imagination, and finally the skills of a loving heart.

9. Develop enthusiasm for the leader's journey.

The journey of a spiritual leader is filled with ups and downs. Sometimes you will think you have arrived at a peak only to find another valley opening up in front of you and realize you have a long way to go. While achievements along the way and other people's encouragement motivate you, the prime support on your journey will always be your own enthusiasm. As we have seen the word "enthusiasm" comes from two Greek words "en theos" meaning "in God." As a spiritual leader you should be enthusiastic about what you are doing, for it is all within the plan and the will of God. The journey will have times of joy and of pain, experiences of enlightenment and of darkness, and occasions of success and of failure. The spiritual leader can embrace all as a part of the commitment he or she makes in faith, hope, and love.

In earlier years I used to climb in the Alps and while the climb would be arduous, exhausting, and even painful, the exhilaration of reaching the peak put everything in perspective. Moreover, once you had reached one peak you became quite accepting of the pain of the climb on other occasions, because you knew what lay ahead and the thrill and satisfaction you would later feel. I think the leader's journey is like this; if he or she keeps the focus on the thrill of the goals of leadership, even the pain can be accepted enthusiastically as part of the whole endeavor. Some leaders and managers fear possible long term failure, become unsure of themselves and cautious in their undertakings. A spiritual leader moves towards a vision of hope and at the same time finds God draws him or her towards the vision. Thus, the perspective is different and enthusiasm a natural response.

A spiritual leader can be enthusiastic for he or she is guided by God and strives to implement the vision of God. The leader can be enthusiastic about co-workers, since in the vision of hope and in appreciation of charismatic community, he or she already accepts their giftedness and their contribution to community. The leader can feel enthusiastic about his or her own leadership because of awareness of having been personally called and endowed with at least some of the talents for leadership. It is almost as if the spiritual leader approaches mission as if it has already been accomplished and so can look back with enthusiasm at the achievements of God through him or her.

As a spiritual leader you should frequently bring to mind your own calling and savor its importance in your own life. When you are enthusiastic about your leadership, your optimism can become contagious and bring enthusiasm to others too. You can look on all you do with enthusiasm, knowing you are immersed "in God—en theos," and can participate in the vision of promise that God offers to humanity. Embrace every aspect of your life as a leader with happiness and profound satisfaction.

10. Clarify the image of God who constantly draws you to leadership.

Much leadership today is without God. Some in leadership positions have hidden from God for so long they have forgotten there is one. People's hopes are silenced by this sort of leadership, and they suffer so much from these leaders they often feel God has abandoned them. Without the influence of God in leaders' lives we live with an incomplete and partial understanding of human dignity, personal destiny, and community values. Spiritual leaders today need to be men and women of God who can live in the presence of God, and whose leadership reflects the faith, hope, and love that come from God.

One of the personal supports for spiritual leaders is their awareness of the presence and call of God. This is not a spectacular occurrence of signs and wonders but an ability to appreciate the small whispers of God's presence in daily events. This skill of finding God and God's will hidden in the daily grind of leadership can have extraordinary impact on one's own leadership and on the people one serves. A spiritual leader can understand the importance of intangibles in life, and see signs of the challenges of God in situations frequently missed by others.

It is important that spiritual leaders do not focus on or present to others an image of God who is too small. Often people drag along behind them an image of God that comes from their earlier life. Others even reject their own image of God because it is too minimal. Our image of God is the single most important aspect of our spiritual lives. The leader must allow two things to happen as he or she struggles within self to find God. First, the leader realizes that God is not like we thought God was. This means re-educating ourselves by letting much of our understanding of God die. We must leave aside images of God as a superboss, oppressive, punisher of failings, unconcerned and distant, a lawgiver, or a male God. To say we believe in God is not enough; far more important is to be clear about the kind of God we believe in. A spiritual leader finds support in a God who is loving, gracious, compassionate, caring, suffering, and forgiving. Former understandings must die and with them certain styles of leadership dependent on them. In their place must emerge a new image of God that challenges to a new way of leading others.

Second, the leader discovers that God often does not act as we thought God would, and this can be a dark experience. Often God does not respond to our needs but calls us to respond ourselves. God is often not a consoler when we need one but a creator of further restlessness. God does not heal when we expect it, but leaves us in pain; does not bring enlightenment but darkness, does not hear our cries but abandons us. This second experience of discovering that God does not act as we expect God to act makes us rethink our image of God and find God is beyond our categories, more than we expected, challenging in ways we never thought of. As a spiritual leader you will find constant support in your understanding of God. The more clearly you experience God the more you can become in some small way an image of the unseen God in your leadership of others.

Spiritual leadership needs supports in order to grow and develop. The world needs spiritual leadership to move to a new dimension of life, peace, and justice for all. If you are called to be this kind of leader then take seriously these and other supports that will enhance your development as a great leader.

STEP EIGHT

EVALUATE YOUR LEADERSHIP: AN ARTIST'S CHALLENGE[1]

I recently returned to Siena, one of the beautiful cities of Tuscany, Italy, to visit the Palazzo Pubblico, the symbol of Siena that presides over its magnificent Piazza del Campo. I had visited this extraordinary building several times, but this time I went to see and reflect on the art in one room in particular, the Sala della Pace (The Hall of Peace), which was the seat of the Government of the Nine who ruled Siena in the 13th to the 14th centuries. In 1337 the Council of Nine commissioned Ambrogio Lorenzetti (1319-1348) to paint their meeting room with a cycle of frescoes, known since 1700 as the Allegories and Effects of Good and Bad Government. Prior to that time the frescoes were simply known as Peace and War. The room is approximately forty-five by twenty-six feet, and Lorenzetti frescoed three walls: the Allegory of Good Government on the north wall, the Effects of Good Government on the east wall, and the Allegory of Bad Government and its Effects on the west wall. Lorenzetti was a man of great learning and culture, "the Artist-Philosopher," and these frescoes

---

[1] The reader may wish to read this chapter alongside the frescoes of Ambrogio Lorenzetti. Several copies of these are available under the title "good and bad government," or under the artist's name "ambrogio lorenzetti." A useful website would be: www.medievalwall.com/painting/ambrogio-lorenzetti-palazzo-publico-siena

evidence his knowledge of Scripture, especially *Revelation*, Aristotelian and Thomistic thought, Augustine's *City of God*, and classical culture and art, notably the political insights of Dante in the *Divine Comedy*. In addition to the artistic and symbolic portrayal, Lorenzetti attaches a written statement in a box, a comment in the frieze, and a banner above, each summarizing the content of the frescos for both good and bad government.

The allegory of Good Government is on the wall directly opposite the window and is lit up by the sun on beautiful days, as well as having its own sources of light in Wisdom and a central sun (now covered over). There are three layers to the fresco. The uppermost has the images of Wisdom and the three theological virtues of Faith, Hope, and Charity, and beside Hope the portrait of the face of Christ. The central layer has the images of Justice, Peace, and the Common Good who is surrounded by Fortitude, Prudence, Magnanimity, Temperance, and Justice. The lower level is presided over by Concord and consists of twenty-four citizens only one of whom is noble, and soldiers, lancers, and prisoners—all part of normal every life.

In addition to the three layers, there are two dynamic developments that tie together the whole fresco. The point of departure for the first is the image of Divine Wisdom who holds the two scales of distributive and commutative justice. Below Wisdom is the Scripture quote; "Love Justice, you who govern the earth." Justice holds the two scales and looks upward to Wisdom. The two angels accompanying Justice pass two cords down to be united in the hand of Concord who has a carpenter's plane on her lap to symbolize the level and equal treatment of all in society. The cord that Concord receives from Justice she then passes on to all twenty-four citizens who hold it in their hands until it is passed on to the hands of Common Good.

The second dynamic development is on the right side of the fresco and begins with the dominating figure of Common Good who is dressed in the colors of Siena and holds its shield. At his feet the wolf suckles the twins—founders of Siena. Above Common Good are the three theological virtues of Faith, Hope, and Charity, while Common Good is accompanied on his long throne by Peace, Fortitude, Prudence, Magnanimity, Temperance, and Justice.

The Effects of Good Government is a fresco on the east wall and shows a people living in peace and harmony, the city's gates wide open, and everyone enjoying the fruits of good government. Above hovers the figure of Security, holding a banner; "Let everyone go without fear, and let everyone sow for as long as Good Government rules, for she has taken power from all the guilty." In the frieze above the fresco are images of spring and summer—the productive times of the year, together with the sun and the kindly planets of Venus and Mercury. Below the fresco are images of the liberal arts, representing the best of natural wisdom.

When you enter the room of the Council of Nine, you immediately come face to face with the darkest part of the room on which Lorenzetti frescoed in dull and gloomy colors the Allegory of Bad Government and its Effects. The central figure is the diabolical tyrant, holding a dagger and a golden cup dripping with blood, for violence and greed are his methods. He has his foot on a goat—symbol of luxury and holds Justice bound beneath him. Above his head the motivating forces of Avarice, Pride, and Vanity (instead of Faith, Hope, and Charity) and accompanying him on his throne a group of vices instead of virtues: Cruelty, Treachery, Fraud, Fury, Discord, and War. The effects of bad government are visible throughout the ruined city with its closed gates, where there is fear, violent crime, robbery, and unproductive land. Above the city hovers the figure of Fear, holding the banner; "Because he seeks his own welfare he subjects justice to tyranny. So, no one walks these roads without fear, for pillage is rife both within and without the city's gates." In the frieze above the fresco are images of the sterile times of the year—autumn and winter, and the unkindly planets of Saturn, Jupiter, and Mars. Below there used to be images of tyrants—only Nero remaining.

Lorenzetti presents us with an artist's rendering of what constitutes good and bad government or good and bad leadership. His fresco is a theology of leadership, a pictorial interpretation of the sources, virtues, essential components of good spiritual leadership, and also evils to be avoided. He does not refer to the obligations of citizens to their rulers, but focuses exclusively on leaders' obligations to those they lead and serve. The Nine may well have seen themselves portrayed in the Allegory of Good Government, but it was there every day they met as both a self-representation and a challenge to the Nine—a reminder to each of them of the values they chose to guide their leadership. After all, few ordinary citizens would ever enter the meeting room of the Nine—this fresco reminds leaders of their duties. The fresco presents a model of leadership and an outstanding tool to evaluate fidelity to the essential components of spiritual leadership. As with any significant artistic representation, the fresco challenges with immediacy. It is not a long drawn out written thesis—it is a picture that focuses your attention on critical values; they are there in front of you and you cannot deny them.

1. Focus always on the common good.

The largest image in the Hall of Peace is Common Good, seen concretely as the embodiment of all those served by dedicated leaders. Everything leaders do must be focused on the Common Good. We live in times of increased factionalism where few leaders seek the common good, emphasizing more the good of their faction while enjoying the defeat of their opponents. A spiritual leader works for the good of the community as a whole without sacrificing the general good for advantages of one individual or group over another. Four images stand out in Lorenzetti's fresco: Common Good, Justice, Concord, and Peace. These four are interrelated in a leader's commitment: emphasizing the common good means above all working for justice, and this commitment produces concord and peace.

Common Good is enthroned below faith, hope, and charity. Faith with a cross looks towards Common Good and reminds onlookers that Jesus died for the common good. Hope looks up to Christ as she yearns for the fruits of his sacrifice in the growth of the common good. Charity looks directly at the audience of the fresco, seeking their response in love for the common good.

The fresco, like leadership, at first seems complex, but a good spiritual leader knows that one must live with a lot of complexity before arriving at simplicity of life. Only one thing is the focus of good leadership, namely the common good. It is a secret that so many contemporary leaders in politics, business, and even religion have forgotten. It is a leader's primary task to give himself or herself to serve the common good through a local institution and through the co-workers in the organization. In any self-evaluation you must ask are you doing good to as many people as possible, do your decisions do harm to some instead of good, do the effects of your leadership reach outward to the community? While a leader's vision is for the universal common good, he or she always realizes it locally. Lorenzetti, while concerned about the common good of humanity, presents the figure in the colors and with the shield of Siena. As a leader you achieve the good you can, but you focus it locally. In the chapters of this book we have seen many components that prepare a leader to give his or her life to the common good. I urge you, as a spiritual leader to never lose sight of this.

1. As a leader, do you seek the common good or do you show favoritism?
2. Do you work as hard for those who do not support you as you do for your supporters?
3. Is your leadership too narrow and provincial, gaining advantage from others' disadvantage?

2. Start from authentic wisdom.

All of Lorenzetti's didactic presentation presumes that Divine Wisdom is the source of good leadership. Clearly he also values human wisdom as we saw in his portrayal of the liberal arts. However, a spiritual leader needs to access divine wisdom. A lot of contemporary leadership suffers from an amputation of spiritual values. We have stressed the need to integrate leadership and spirituality, to emphasize the Christian dimensions of leadership, and to make time for reflection and prayer. We have stressed that this world's values are not enough, that leaders must seek transformation, and that they are called to implement a vision of hope. Above all we have seen that spiritual leaders align their vision with their values, that they seek enlightenment from a strong personal faith, and that they need to be guided by their image of God. We have summed up many of these challenges by saying simply that a leader lives on two horizons of life at the same time—here and now and there and then. Leaders today in whatever ways they choose must understand that leadership starts from authentic wisdom, and that is a gift of God. So, this figure of

Lorenzetti is the point of departure for the whole fresco. From wisdom comes justice, from justice comes concord, from concord comes the common good. Seeking to develop the latter three while omitting the first will get a leader nowhere. Wisdom is not earned, it is a gift. So, as a leader you must find ways of being open to divine wisdom. This will include prayer and contemplation, study and reflection, discussion with like-minded leaders, an ability to foster a sense of mystery and awe in your own life, and courage to speak about these values without embarrassment.

Lorenzetti is insistent that divine wisdom be complemented by the best of human wisdom, and so he places the liberal arts in the lower frieze. In the thought of the time, natural wisdom prepares us for divine wisdom. Some contemporary leaders are just too ignorant to be good leaders. They may be technologically skilled and managerially gifted, but leadership deals with human beings in their longings and hopes. A leader needs to be a wise person, and this certainly includes the liberal arts, philosophy, theology, literature, and history. It is difficult to seek the good of humanity when you do not know what it is. Obviously this does not mean every leader needs to be outstanding in these areas, but there needs to be an awareness of human knowledge if a leader is to have a transforming impact on others.

1. Do you appreciate that Divine Wisdom is the authentic source of your leadership?

2. What do you do to open your mind and heart to God's will for your leadership?

3. Are you an educated and cultured leader who also values the best in human wisdom?

3. Remember the foundations of leadership.

On the same level as Divine Wisdom, Lorenzetti places the three theological virtues of Faith, Hope, and Love. Faith carries a cross, Hope looks confidently upward toward the face of Christ, and Charity carries a heart and an arrow as symbols of love of God and of neighbor. These are the three foundations for striving for the common good. They are theological virtues not moral; in other words they are three aspects of God's transforming life within us that motivate us in all we do. They go together and center on love.

Leaders have faith in love, they hope that love will not be lost, and they center all they do on love for the common good. We have addressed each of these three values in the earlier chapters of this book. These are not three skills, but three energies of one's inner spirit. In Lorenzetti's fresco they are part of the highest layer that refers to transcendent values. In this vision, faith is a gift of God and is greater than accumulated knowledge. Hope is a gift and is greater than all accumulated memories. Charity is a gift and is greater than all accumulated desires. These three qualities guide a leader in his or her vision of life, of the common good, and of the goals of leadership.

Like wisdom, these energies of the inner spirit are not earned, they are given to those people who prepare themselves and are open and receptive. Rather than three actions of a leader, they are three aspects of the transformation that God brings to chosen leaders. The most we can do is to prepare ourselves to receive these gifts, and we have focused on the appropriate preparations in the earlier part of the book. Perhaps the easiest way to evaluate oneself on these foundations is to look at the effects of good leadership in one's own life. Lorenzetti's fresco of secure life in city and countryside presents a vision that is built on faith, responds to hope, and is permeated with love. A glance at the effects of bad government shows us community life that is faithless, hopeless, and loveless.

1. Give examples of how faith, hope, and love motivate you as a leader.
2. In what ways does the transforming action of God come into your life?
3. How does your leadership differ from someone else's who has no faith, hope, or love?

4. Enthrone justice.

Justice appears twice in the fresco. Seated alongside Common Good, Justice is a cardinal virtue. On the left side of the fresco Justice is the incarnation of divine wisdom, and she looks up to Wisdom to guide her in all she does. An inscription on the lower border of the fresco proclaims, "Wherever this holy virtue of Justice rules, she leads many to unity, and these, so united, make up the Common Good." The praise of Justice continues along the lower border of the fresco on the Effects of Good Government. "Turn your eyes, you who rule, to look at Justice. . . . She always give each man his rightful due. . . how sweet life is and full of peace. . . where this virtue is to be seen." Justice touches the scales that measure out justice, although they are held in balance by Wisdom. Justice cannot achieve much without the tension to good and evil that comes from Wisdom. In recent years, politicians and business professionals all over the world have shown how degraded their leadership becomes without justice. At times we wonder if they can fall any lower in their greed, selfishness, and lack of concern for justice and the poor. We desperately need leaders inspired by justice.

In previous chapters we have reviewed the failures of leadership, asked contemporary leaders to do no harm, and urged readers to set a new direction in their leadership. We have asked that leaders give hope, confront with compassion, and build positive relationships with all. This means knowing how to make ethical judgments, having a model of ethical decision-making, and monitoring carefully the implications of one's decisions on others. Justice needs hard work, and it is very much influenced by wisdom, by one's understanding of the vision of hope that comes from making judgments in light of a realm of life beyond this one. Put simply a leader needs to make decisions in this life in light of his or her own death and the judgment of the horizon of life beyond this one.

It is sad that the fresco of the effects of bad government describe so many contemporary leaders who lack justice. Let us hope that readers of this book will be willing to give themselves to the care of those they serve, to create just environments and policies for those who work with them, to produce products that do no harm and that contribute positively to others' lives, and to create models of justice for others to admire.

1. Do your co-workers recognize you as a just person?
2. What kinds of organizational structures have you developed to guarantee justice?
3. How does justice in your organization lead others to unity?

5. Work for concord.

Unlike Wisdom and Justice who look heavenward, Concord looks towards the citizens and Common Good. She passes the cord that comes from Justice and holds her carpenter's plane to symbolize equality and fairness. Concord is presented in very human form, down-to earth, and deals with the real issues of establishing unity. "Concord," does not refer to the cord that she received from justice and passes on to all the citizens. Rather, "concord," comes from Latin and means "being of one heart;" it refers to efforts to build agreement and to avoid all forms of bitterness and rivalry. Concord is the binding force of society and removes factionalism and internal strife. In the thought of the day, justice and the common good guaranteed peace and concord. In this book we have often addressed the issues of unity and community, and detailed ways in which a spiritual leader creates an environment that reflects respect, appreciation, even reverence for others' contributions to a common cause. Building concord is a precious skill of a spiritual leader who knows that little is achieved by lonely individuals but that much is by those united in mind and heart. Comparing the two frescos of good and bad government is like listening to Martin Luther King Jr.'s assessment that hatred paralyzes life but love releases it, hatred confuses life whereas love harmonizes it, and hatred darkens life but love illumines it. A leader who builds love and concord passes on those values to all the citizens and thence to Common Good who treasures concord above almost everything else.

Concord is a quality of community that we have lost, and instead we frequently see divisiveness, polarization, egoism, and even an unwillingness to make effort to appreciate other people's point of view. This infects politics, business, religion, family life, and professional development. Today's spiritual leaders must be prophets of the value of concord and strive ceaselessly to build it.

1. Are you known for fairness and equality in your dealings with co-workers?
2. Specify what you do to build concord and remove bitterness in your organization.

3. What signs of factionalism and internal strife do you see in your organization and what can you do about them?

6. Seek peace.

Peace is one of the most extraordinary figures in the fresco. Presented as a beautiful woman, she looks towards Common Good. Peace is resting, sitting on top of a pile of armory from a former war; although calm, she is alert and vigilant. Peace is situated at the center of the fresco, and at one time the sun was directly above her. The pursuit of justice and the common good lead to peace. When we watch the television or look at the newspapers it can be very depressing to see so much war locally in families and among co-workers, nationally among competing groups whose viciousness to each other is overwhelming, and internationally where dictators randomly murder to keep themselves in power and wealth. Sometimes we long to get away from something like this but do not know exactly what we are looking for. When a viewer first looks at Lorenzetti's fresco, one image stands out, Peace. Unlike all the others, she is in white, looks very relaxed, and holds the olive branch. It is not enough to be peaceful in oneself, and towards others, leaders today must be peacemakers. What preceded her calm attentiveness is not immediately clear, but she is seated on weapons of former wars, and a glance at the effects of bad government will remind us of just what she has had to do to get to this point of watchfulness.

A leader knows that there are serious threats to peace in all levels of organizational life. Division, tensions, confrontations, hostility, and serious conflicts are not only everywhere in the fresco of the effects of bad government but in the organizations in which we work. So much so, that we often anxiously wonder if peace is attainable anymore. As Lorenzetti wrote on his fresco, quoting Scripture, there is no peace without justice. This means a spiritual leader must work constantly for respect of human rights, for conscience formation among all the workers, for training in conflict resolution, and for ongoing reform of organizational structures so that they more readily express the peace the leader seeks. At the same time a leader must make sure that peace is not threatened by uncertainty, doubt, or suspicion. Rather he or she needs to cultivate good communications, dialogue, community building skills, and reconciliation. Moreover, a spiritual leader who longs to establish a vision of peace and become a builder of peace should not neglect the simple gestures of peace, a language of peace, team-building, and encounters of friendship. Every day you must remind yourself that good leadership has at its center the figure of Peace.

1. Are you and your organization known for generating peace?
2. How can peaceful attitudes help you and your organization to be more productive?
3. Do you hope for peace or work for it? Specify.

7. Embody the appropriate virtues.

Alongside Common Good sit six virtues: the four cardinal virtues, so-called because the moral and political life of society hinge on these four values ("cardinal" comes from the Latin for hinge), and added to these are Peace and Magnanimity. Lorenzetti's inscription below the fresco reminds Common Good that he must keep his eyes fixed on these six qualities. Next to Peace is Fortitude who holds a sword and shield, symbols of strength. Then comes Prudence who holds a scroll on which is written "past, present, and future," to remind Common Good to learn from the past, be aware of opportunities in the present, and look to new possibilities in the future. On the immediate left of Common Good is Magnanimity who holds a crown and a bowl of precious stones to indicate the need in the leader of a big heart capable of grand gestures that overcome the meanness of lesser leaders. Rather, she thinks of the welfare of all. Next to Magnanimity is Temperance holding an hour-glass as a warning to use time well. Finally, sits Justice who distributes justice and punishment with fairness. These are six virtues that govern life in community. A spiritual leader must excel in these qualities.

We have mentioned these values previously, and we have already looked at Peace and Justice. Fortitude is a key value for a spiritual leader; the courage and determination to stay with the commitment made, the challenge to re-discover great leadership, and the call to make it part of one's life is a daily task. It includes accepting the pain of leadership, dealing with crises, pursuing the best you can be, and living one's vision of leadership with perseverance. Prudence is the virtue of exercising sound judgment when faced with alternatives. It enables a leader to evaluate what is good in the past, the present, and the future so as to capitalize on all that is good for the benefit of others. It regulates the decisions and actions of a leader, enabling him or her to make good decisions, and so prudence implies skills of evaluation, insight, and foresight. On the left of Common Good is Magnanimity. Unfortunately, this is a little-used word today. However, it is a wonderful word to describe a leader, for it refers to a person who has a big spirit or a big heart. Such leaders give themselves generously to others; constantly seek to respect and understand others, and to appreciate their goodness. A magnanimous leader is non-judgmental, excels in listening to the input of others, and always has a place in his or her heart for others whether agreeing with them or not. Sitting next to Magnanimity is Temperance, the virtue by which we govern with moderation all we do, think, or feel. It is the virtue that controls all forms of excess. Like the other three cardinal virtues it is a super-virtue which influences the way we live all other aspects of life. It is a delightful quality, which has been absent from so many contemporary leaders. A spiritual leader seeks to be prudent in all he or she does.

1. Give examples of where the four cardinal virtues are present in your leadership.
2. Magnanimity is worth a special mention. Are you big hearted and capable of grand gestures for the good of others?
3. In which of these six virtues do you excel and in which are you weak?

8. Check the effects of good leadership.

From one's fruits you will know whether someone lives good leadership or not. The fresco on the east wall, the Effects of Good Government, is in two parts separated by the city wall. On the left are the effects of good government on city life, and on the right the effects of good government on life in the countryside.

Above hovers Security with her consoling words, and on the border below Lorenzetti points to the peace, security, and enjoyable aspects of life under good leadership. People in all walks of life go about their work, family life, and social interactions in security and peace. The scene is permeated with harmony, within the city and countryside and between the two as people move freely and celebrate the activities of their daily lives. Life is good for those who benefit from good leadership. The leaders themselves are nowhere to be seen except in the effects their leadership produces.

As a spiritual leader you need to assess the outcomes of your leadership. You can do this personally, or you can get someone else to do it for you and your organization. You can have all the plans in the world to be a good spiritual leader, but only the fruits of your endeavors show the success or failure. In previous chapters we have suggested that your leadership ought to give the world something to think about, that you should examine your life constantly, that you must check to see that you are striving to be the best you can be, and that it is your responsibility to maintain the dream for others. When you look at the fruits of your leadership you should be able to identify the prophetical, mystical, charismatic, and healing effects of what you have done. Certainly as a leader you must spread the message, create a trusting environment, and have a transforming impact on your organization. Many individuals who think they are good leaders have little to show for it. As a spiritual leader you must frequently review the effects of your leadership. As Lorenzetti says in the lower border, just look at how many good effects come from a leader who is dedicated to the right values. May you be such a one.

1. If people look at the effects of your leadership what kind of a leader would they think you to be?

2. Is the working environment you have created more reflective of the fresco on Good Government or Bad Government?

3. For Lorenzetti, the effects of good leadership are expansive and spread way beyond the initial organization. Do yours?

9. Avoid all forms of Tyranny.

The west wall of the Council of Nine's meeting room has one fresco that combines the three parts of the previous frescos— bad government, its effects on city life, and its effects of life in the countryside. Tyranny has overcome justice, and war and discord replace peace and concord. The town is closed and destruction and death are everywhere in the city, the countryside is barren. Lorenzetti contrasts every aspect of good government with the defects, hatred, and fear of this fresco. In the lower border, Lorenzetti has written, "Where Justice is bound no one struggles for the Common Good . . .but rather permits the rise of Tyranny. . . [who] persecutes those who wish to do good and attracts all who plan evil." At the feet of Tyranny Justice lies bound on the floor. Above the head of Tyranny instead of the theological virtues we find Pride with a dagger and abandoned yoke—the symbol of humility, Avarice with a harpoon and two bags of money, and Vanity as a beautiful young woman looking at herself in a mirror and holding a withered branch. This fresco corresponds to our own experiences of life today. How can we cover the abyss of tyranny in its many forms today?

Political leaders have tyrannized their own nations and people, using oppression, imprisonment, murder, and rape to control and terrorize their own people. Business parasites have laid waste the life savings of millions to maintain their own power, prestige, and life-style. Organizations at all levels of society are so filled with corruption, we have to say it is systemic in many countries and in many professions. All problems of leadership begin with pride. Tyranny places his feet on the goat of luxury, surrounds himself with evil-minded dependents, and allows others to commit evil at will, provided they support his need for control. "Tyranny persecutes those who wish to do good, and attracts all those who plan evil. It always defends those who use force, or rob, or hate peace." We look at our world that Lorenzetti seems to be describing, and we know how much we need great spiritual leaders. May at least a small percentage of readers accept the call.

    1.   Are there any traces of pride, avarice, or vanity in your leadership?

2. Tyranny is the clearest indicator of failed leadership, give examples of how this evil has been present in your own life and leadership.
3. Do you ever find yourself looking in the mirror to admire your own achievements instead of focusing on others?

10. Watch for the signs of bad leadership.

The bad leadership, Tyranny, is surrounded with six vices that replace the six virtues of Good Government. Cruelty who torments a baby with a snake, Treachery who holds a lamb that has a scorpion's tale, and Fraud who has bat's wings and claws. There on the left of Tyranny we see Fury presented as a centaur with an animal's head holding a stone and a dagger, Discord or division in a dress on half of which is written "yes" and on the other half "no," and holds a saw to cut unevenly rather than Concord's plane, and finally War as a soldier in the act of killing. City and countryside are filled with crime, hate, and unhappiness, while above hovers the figure of Fear. The city of bad government is closed with only soldiers free to enter or leave. Everyone is a slave to the needs of the tyrant. Many leaders who disgust us today did not become as they are overnight. They gradually lost values, pursued selfish interests, lost sight of others' needs, and ended up lonely and diabolical. How many so-called leaders today are filled with pride, avarice, and vanity. Most evenings our television news focuses on cruelty, treachery, fraud, fury, discord, and war. We live in a sad world, deprived of great spiritual leaders. Look at some of the hateful and hate-filled men and women of the beginning of the twenty-first century, immerse yourself in sorrow at their decadence, be aware you can also fail, and then humbly renew your commitment to the vocation to serve the common good.

1. Cruelty, treachery, fraud, fury, discord, and war—any signs of these evils in your organization?
2. Does fear or security hover over your administration?
3. What would you identify as your significant weaknesses as a leader?

Lorenzetti's fresco stimulates thoughts of then and now, dreams and reality, our hopes and our fears. What would be your fresco, or image, or collage of good and bad leadership? Which images from modern artists—painters, poets, writers, musicians—affect you, challenging you in the styles of leadership you feel called to live and to avoid?

STEP NINE

WORK WITH YOUR FOLLOWERS-DISCIPLES

Our focus throughout this book has been on the personal life of the leader. In this chapter too, we are not primarily concerned with the techniques and skills of working with others but how the spiritual leader's personal life develops through working with others who form a community of followers and disciples around the leader. A great spiritual leader will find that disciples gather to learn how to become similar leaders.

1. Spread the message.

Among the most fundamental responsibilities of a spiritual leader are to always be good at what he or she does as an administrator; to maintain competence, to develop new skills as needed, to keep up-to-date and up-to-par in all that relates to being an outstanding and responsible leader. However, if you have dedicated yourself to some or all of the steps and recommendations we have reflected on together in this book, then you will want to share your vision of leadership with those with whom you work and with others too beyond your organization. Your own call and vision enthuse you and fill you with desire to share them with others. In this way you extend your own approach to leadership through others; you extend your vision and influence as you gather around you men and women of like-mind. As you spread these values through others you become a witness to the truth of life in community, of leadership through service, of growth through quality interaction, and of the power of a vision of hope. Spreading the message of transformative leadership is a leader's participation in evangelization—the spreading of the gospel message.

A great spiritual leader becomes a lover of leadership development, as he or she prolongs and extends vision and mission through others. This further understanding of leadership leads to a new discovery about oneself, a new sense of mission and purpose in life; namely, to lead others to a vision eventually implies leading others to lead themselves. Being a leader is not easy and sharing the message requires humility, since others will consider you the initial source of vision. However, you need to do what you are called to do to lead and to create leaders who extend the vision. Great spiritual leaders always become teachers of leadership, willingly sharing their values and vision, and seeking to fill others with enthusiasm to become spiritual leaders.

Spiritual leadership is the result of personal transformation; it is the integration of leadership skills and vision with personal spiritual growth. So, when you seek to share your vision of spiritual leadership you are not only passing on to followers the instrumental, interpersonal, immaginal, and system skills of leadership, but you are also drawing others to personal spiritual renewal and growth. Thus, you will need to communicate your own appreciation for the vision of hope, the will of God, the call to prayer, the need of conversion, and the challenges of living faith, hope, and love. This will require of you special skills since you are a leader with organizational responsibilities not a preacher. However, calmly and inconspicuously you can and must share the deep values of your inner spirit. Eventually, you create around yourself a community of followers dedicated to the pursuit of spiritual leadership.

2. Channel others' gifts.

When others follow your leadership their own call should also emerge. Part of the responsibility of working with followers is to learn how to channel their gifts. This requires that you maintain good personal relationships with each one, finding out what special talents and competencies each one has. We have seen that a spiritual leader sees his or her organization as a charismatic community and appreciates every person has a gift or gifts to share. The leader must release followers' potential and become a clearinghouse for their gifts—identifying, channeling, and capitalizing on each one's contribution. The spiritual leader must create in followers a sense of purpose, fostering their initiative, giving visibility to their know-how, and reinforcing good performance. The leader can create work assignments that bring out the best in followers, letting them see and appreciate their own gifts, and being surprised at their own success. The spiritual leader will involve followers in something they have never done before and let them then identify in themselves new skills not seen previously.

An important way of channeling others' gifts is through delegation, when the leader gives followers some authority over tasks that need to be done, so they can develop their own leadership potential. The leader must delegate something significant, not something the leader does not want to do. While the leader retains overall responsibility, followers begin to discover their own leadership potential through delegation. The spiritual leader can then seek feedback from followers and evaluate the results of delegation, identifying successes and failures, seeing skills that became evident and others that need fostering, and reviewing how leadership was present or absent.

A further way of channeling others' gifts is through collaboration when the leader moves beyond delegation to working with followers as partners in a common undertaking. The leader can set up pilot projects which can only be effective when all members of a team work together, each one having authority over part of the project. Collaboration is a practical expression of equality and shared responsibility. It presupposes a common shared vision, an ability to dialogue, mutual respect and support, and a willingness to accept the full participation of all members of a team. People will not do things in the way others might prefer, but that is part of the learning experience of working together.

A spiritual leader knows he or she can achieve much more by utilizing others' gifts than by leading on his or her own. If the leader brings everyone into the project the members can learn from each other, appreciate each other's gifts, and find new levels of satisfaction and productivity. Like many new ventures, collaboration takes time at the beginning, but as the experience develops, it produces excellent results in synergy and the fusion of gifts. It will also call you to develop your own leadership through this enriching interaction with others.

3. Support co-workers and followers.

A spiritual leader always wants to have a positive impact on followers and seeks to be supportive of them in any way possible. Some will feel supported by a smile, forms of respect, a gesture of kindness, signs of friendship. A spiritual leader must evidence genuine benevolence to followers, thinking well of them even before they ever do anything. The leader stresses good communication, approachability, and an openness for understanding. Followers need to know you respect them, appreciate them, and like them—all contribute to an awareness of your support. You can be supportive by emphasizing their dignity more than your own, by being yourself and not claiming position and status, by removing special perks reserved for the leadership elite. You can also be supportive of followers by being constantly visible and available. On occasions you can also support others by controlling or removing the odd or eccentric individuals in the organization as well as the permanent critics and gripers who can be so unsupportive.

A further way of supporting followers is to create a pleasant working environment. This will include speaking with courtesy and pleasantness, sharing significant information, promoting open dialogue, and giving full attention to their questions. A spiritual leader will try to give followers what they need. When possible it is helpful to create schedules more conducive to followers' daily needs. As a spiritual leader you will always treat followers fairly in all matters relating to their work—positions, salaries, promotions, evaluations, and so on. Respecting their rights, competencies, levels of authority, duties, and achievements is also a responsibility. A spiritual leader will focus his or her support on the whole person of a follower, appreciating the need for support of physical, working, emotional, moral, and spiritual aspects of life.

You show support when you engage in joint efforts with your followers, encourage them in their development, interact with constant patience, forgive them readily for failure while evaluating opportunities for change and improvement. By affirming others, fostering a spirit of solidarity, and raising followers' dignity by asking them for help and seeking their feedback on important projects you demonstrate the quality of your leadership. It is of the utmost importance that a spiritual leader appreciates followers' pride in their work and in themselves, and that he or she respect and affirm it. Followers of a good spiritual leader know they are supported and even know they are loved.

A leader who supports followers will find they will give more of themselves, will identify more specifically with a common endeavor and shared values, and will find more satisfaction in their work. When a leader can integrate a supportive approach to work with a supportive commitment to personal spiritual development, followers find a deeper meaning in life, and what they learn at work influences the whole of their lives.

4. Find ways to teach the people who work with you.

Spiritual leaders find that they are surrounded by followers who want to learn from them. "Disciple" is a word that means to learn, and the spiritual leader discovers that he or she truly has disciples who aspire to be great leaders too. Teaching is often easier to accept when it is indirect and informal, and when it arises from the normal events of each day. Above all a leader teaches by example, by being a role model of the vision and values of authentic leadership. As a spiritual leader, you can let your presence and commitment reveal the true meaning of life and the vocation of leadership. As we have seen the first level of teaching by example is to educate followers to be competent. Clearly, followers learn more from watching a good leader in action than from books or workshops. Beyond the extremely important skills of competence, good management, and leadership, followers can appreciate the spiritual leader's values, conscience formation, and inner spirit, and this adds the dimension of spiritual growth.

A spiritual leader turns the organization in to a school of values, of leadership, and of service. Giving priority to ethics throughout the organization aids followers in their moral training. Moreover, when the organization under the direction of a spiritual leader trains the whole person and insists on balance and perspective in life, then followers can keep working life in check and in perspective regarding their family and friendship groups, so that work does not absorb life and so that followers' wider human needs can be satisfied. Within the context of organizational life a leader needs to teach followers a new understanding of commitment, so that they can move beyond professional dedication to discretionary commitment whereby they give of themselves beyond professional expectations. In fact, the leader needs to be able to motivate followers to motivate themselves.

Through example and sharing—both informal and formal, a spiritual leader initiates followers to an appreciation of two horizons of life—that of daily activity and then the horizon of life beyond this one that gives meaning to this one. Leadership that leaves spiritual values behind is always incomplete, and the leader who wishes to emphasize the transforming value of human activity will insist on adding a vision of faith to the partial truths and understandings of leadership. The leader's teaching responsibility eventually includes challenging followers to appreciate the prophetical, charismatic, mystical, and healing tasks of leadership. Teaching culminates in aiding followers to perceive the transforming effects of a leadership that is permeated by faith, hope, and love. Every leader should ask himself or herself is there anything special about my leadership that others could learn.

While teaching can be achieved informally, it does not exclude formal input from the leader. Followers can be deeply impressed by a leader's example and learn much in this way. However, sometimes it is also valuable to see connections and reasons for one's leadership choices, to appreciate how a variety of insights learned from a leader's example come together in an integrated vision of leadership. Again formal input can explain why a leader does what he or she does, and how leadership values relate to each other.

5. Make sure co-workers know how important they are.

Part of leadership is to welcome followers' gifts, to give them every support you can, and to appreciate what they do for the organization. However, you must go beyond these approaches and make sure followers know how important they are. It does not matter at what level in the organization a person is, it is important that everyone knows that he or she is a very important part of the success of the whole enterprise. Max Dupree tells of setting up a statue of a water-carrier in one office building as a symbol of everyone's importance. Although the man only carried water, in his village water was the most important aspect of village life. Spiritual leaders appreciate the importance of all persons for who they are and then for what they contribute to the whole community. Importance does not come from position or possessions, but from being a person of integrity and from personal dedication to the common work of the group—CEO, office cleaner, manager, secretary, technician, cook—you must make sure they all know they are important members of the organization.

Each person who works for you must feel he or she is handpicked. As a spiritual leader you will pay attention to each one, listen carefully to their input, be attentive to them, even taking notes when they speak. You must let them know you need them, acknowledge their talents and achievements, and never steal recognition due to them. There is a way in which a leader reverences followers and they know it.

A spiritual leader stresses the importance of every follower by drawing out each one's own leadership. No longer prisoners of old leadership styles, we now all have a common calling to serve others. So, the leader carefully considers followers' views, not as a technique to give the impression of importance but as the result of a deep conviction on the goodness and giftedness of each one. A great leader asks followers to be more successful than they are or ever expected to be. Followers' surprise at being viewed as so important can transform their lives and the quality of their dedication to the organization.

As we have seen in other sections, a spiritual leader constantly keeps an eye on the development of the whole person.

Thus, the leader keeps interest in each one, and expresses genuine concern and friendship for followers and their families. A leader can also stress followers' importance by investing in their training, so that they each know the organization is looking forward and expecting much from them in the future. The leader encourages followers to share their experiences concerning the organization and its mission. In this way the shared vision can be strengthened with the experiences, evaluations, and interpretations of each one. What a spiritual leader particularly wants is that each follower becomes his or her authentic self, for such followers contribute immensely to the development of the organization, and then everyone can see how truly important they are.

6. Build a trusting environment.

A leader knows that without trust there is no likelihood of growth in community spirit or commitment to a shared mission. A spiritual leader creates a working environment of mutual trust in which people relying on the integrity and authenticity of others always have confident expectations that they will act according to their own values and truth. Trust becomes the emotional glue that binds people together and lets them act as if information is reliable, as if people are competent and motivated, even without solid evidence. This is risky, but trust grows in proportion to our ability to risk, and as people become more reliable they earn trust. When trust is present in an organization, collaboration and partnership are possible, people are free to become their best selves, and vision and mission grow in shared solidarity. The spiritual leader who wishes to create an environment of trust must be dependable, deserving of confidence, reliable, faithful, believable, and always seen to be honest and just—these are the reasons for trust.

Building a trusting environment is always a challenge. It starts with the conviction and hope that others share our concerns and respect our competence. It also means that we have similar interests to build quality relationships, to improve the experience of organizational life, and to foster institutional outcomes. The spiritual leader always highlights the positive, respects followers' freedom, and handles mistakes with care, respect, and ongoing challenge. Treating others as partners, relying on their gifts, and acknowledging that success depends on everyone working together is essential. Fear in the community is deadly, so the leader must eliminate it. Being flexible and ready to compromise to reach consensus, and being unthreatened by other people's competence and strengths also follows. The spiritual leader is willing to live with ambiguity and tension, fosters critical thinking and, when differences arise, realizes that anger and love are not mutually exclusive. Trust is the commitment of adult and mature people, and it strengthens the organization's life and effectiveness.

As a spiritual leader you will work to gain people's respect. They will expect integrity, competence, fairness, and realism from you in your daily work. They will look to you for a clear commitment to the organization's vision and for every effort to make it real. Each one will want you to be accepting, caring, and open to them and their ideas. These requisites will at times imply appropriate self-revelation, quality presence to others, and a spirit of equality in your treatment of followers. Building a trusting environment is demanding, but trust creates more trust, and thus the organization grows to the benefit of all.

7. Oversee co-workers' development.

A spiritual leader respects the privacy of all workers; when they leave in the evening or at weekend, each one has a personal story and life. However, work is a major component of everyone's human experience, and what we learn at work impacts every aspect of our lives. It offers us the basic expression of human creativity and the normal way of self-realization. In transforming their work, men and women transform themselves. Admittedly, work is hard, but the struggle brings satisfaction, a sense of achievement, often health through exercise, and awareness of being needed. Work leads to personal growth, family support, and social benefits. A spiritual leader knows that what takes place during working hours can enrich every aspect of a person's life, and so the leader has opportunity to oversee followers' development in ways few others do. Maybe a worker goes to Church or a religious function once a week—generally lasting about one hour. However, he or she spends around forty hours a week at work. The leader can never be paternalistic or maternalistic—those times are passed, but he or she can help develop qualities in workers, aware that they can transform every aspect of their lives. Whether workers develop their senses, or channel their emotions, or focus their intellectual development, they have opportunities to constantly act as adults in interaction with others. A leader can aid followers in learning to plan, in setting up a solid vision, and in training for insight and enlightenment. As followers work with and for others, they learn mutual service and catch glimpses of the meaning of life. The leader gives them opportunities for development, promoting them when merited, and even celebrating their departure when it is for something better for them.

A leader can challenge followers to continuous improvement. He or she can provide opportunities to followers for greatness beyond their expectations and insist on evaluation and redirection. In doing so the leader encourages risk taking, gives and receives feedback, and challenges followers to the personal fulfillment for which they yearn. All these qualities impact followers' entire development and pay high dividends at work, at home, and throughout community. Once a leader assigns work, men and women increasingly act on their own initiative and judgment regarding human moral values at work. The immediacy of decision making at work demands maturity of conscience, courage to make rapid decisions, humility to live with mistakes, and enough trust not to be discouraged. The demands of work today force people into very delicate situations with difficult ethical and socio-ethical consequences, and leaders must educate followers in these situations too, knowing this also will impact life in general. While a good leader keeps the focus on working situations and avoids any interference with a worker's private life, there is no doubt that a spiritual leader can indirectly influence the worker's integrated development; for one's personality is formed especially during the hours of work. Thus, a leader throughout his or her service of others at work can oversee quality change that impacts the whole of a worker's life. It is extraordinary what a good leader can do.

8. Confront with compassion.

Followers contribute so much to the community but at times also fail or fall short of expectations at work. A spiritual leader knows that some failure without reprimand is good, and not all failures need to be pointed out to workers or always criticized. Workers often see their own mistakes, evaluate them, and correct them, without any input from management. If a leader needs to criticize the failings of a follower, he or she should do so, generally in private, with compassion, and constructively, so that failure becomes a learning experience and an occasion to strengthen relationships and mutual respect. In these situations a leader needs to be known as a person who has the courage to speak the truth. He or she must be proactive and not wait until problems are too great to be resolved constructively. Intervening earlier, challenging with compassion, reprimanding with firmness, the leader deals with problems with gentleness and always constructively. The spiritual leader should mourn with those who have failed but through constructive criticism draw good out of the negativity. Throughout the needed criticism, the leader must maintain clear priorities—respect, improvement, growth, and unity.

At times problems can arise in the group, and the leader must utilize the skills of conflict management. Constructive conflict is a sign of organizational vitality. Admittedly, at times some conflict does not lead to growth; friction festers and degenerates into unresolved anger. However, a spiritual leader who constantly supports and encourages followers must also challenge them and must deal with conflict when it arises. The leader can best deal with conflict when he or she has established good relationships with everyone involved and has trained followers to appreciate that conflict is an integral part of growth. All involved must be willing to work for a resolution to the crisis and accept the reality of the need of change. Having worked hard to build a good community spirit and a healthy working environment, leader and followers must focus on facts and never on other people's motives. All need to be ready to resolve the conflict speedily, work for a win-win outcome, forget the disagreement, and bear no grudges. Strategic conflict is an opportunity for growth, can help followers understand each other more, reinforces the self-esteem of all, and channels different opinions into the community's mutual understanding.

A spiritual leader creates a healthy organization in which members generally seek solutions together. This will never exclude the need for direct involvement by the leader at times. Resolving disputes and confronting with compassion is most effective when the leader has already developed the points discussed in this chapter: everyone's gifts are known and celebrated, there is a supportive spirit throughout the organization, the leader accepts his or her teaching responsibility, all followers know the importance of everyone to the common good, there is a trusting environment, and the leader shows great care in fostering the development of all. In such an organization each follower can leave aside personal agendas, respond without fear, and contribute collaboratively in times of criticism and conflict.

9. Lead followers to personal transformation.

Some leaders give their followers adequate information and skills to get the job done. Such workers are judged on their efficiency, they know how to do the job, and they do what they do for their own sakes. They have obligation to themselves to keep the job and must respond to the will of the boss. Some leaders go a little further than this job training and foster different actions and behaviors in their workers, so that they strive to do the job as well as possible. Such workers are judged on their excellence and respond to the firm's challenge to quality, and they do what they do as part of the organization's goals to which they feel responsible. Other leaders focus on the experiences and attitudes of followers, urging them to reflect values in their decision-making at work. Such workers judge themselves on their contribution to the organization's shared values and mission and feel responsible to the common good. A spiritual leader calls followers to reflect on their purpose in life, their destiny, to know why they do what they do, and to feel responsible to ultimate values as part of their reason for existence.

Spiritual leaders are not satisfied with providing followers with information, skills, improvement, and attitudinal development—they certainly do all this, but they want to move their co-workers to transformation. Thus, followers develop a different approach to what they do, to what they see themselves achieving in life. Transformation is like a conversion, even working life is viewed in light of ultimate values of goodness, justice, and love. Job training, organizational culture, even mission values yield to approaches to life that come out of a vision of hope, God's will for the world, commitments made in light of faith, hope, and love.

Transformation implies a better way of living and means a person can see beyond the task. The individual is caught up in a mission and vision beyond daily work, a participant in serving the common good and in influencing the world with values of a vision of hope for humanity. This is not esoteric or beyond the concerns of average workers. Many nurses or doctors not only see the patient to whom they give care but can see themselves involved in a mission of healing for humanity. A bricklayer not only builds a wall but a cathedral. A teacher not only gives information but has a vision of culture and education for the world. They and many like them are all interested in being a part of something more than average, something beyond the narrow confines of their work or profession.

As a spiritual leader you strive for followers' transformation but have no control over it. Co-workers gain an energy of their own, beyond what you at first expected. Transformation means you urge people to move to a point where they no longer need you. That is why we do not see many transformative leaders. When you seek the transformation of workers, then you have to accept new challenges when you find you are no longer needed as before. Transformation takes courageous hope.

10. Give followers freedom and let them go.

A leader guarantees freedom to co-workers, freedom to be themselves and to express their opinions on issues of importance to the organization. The leader needs to remove any fear in the community, so that workers feel free to express their criticism and even challenge the leader's own approaches to issues. Then, through delegation and collaboration the leader gives followers authority to make their own decisions. However, this freedom is not something that just happens. Rather, it is part of community building that a leader facilitates. People are not free to be involved in organizational development unless they are also free of prejudice, misleading information, apathy, lack of reflection, unwillingness to change, and so on. Educating people to freedom takes time and effort. A spiritual leader enables freedom among co-workers as part of community building.

When a leader has coached followers well, then he or she must give greater freedom and responsibility to them. The leader must stop making all the decisions, provide adequate information, and then give greater discretion to followers. This means getting out of their way and letting them feel in charge. This also implies removing unnecessary rules and regulations that put controls on others' initiative, and restraining yourself from constantly involving yourself in what followers can do well on their own. A spiritual leader accepts subsidiarity as a common practice—letting decisions be made at the lowest level at which they can appropriately be made. This kind of freedom creates responsibility among co-workers.

It often happens that a good leader trains followers in every way possible, leading them to genuine transformation, shared responsibility, and their own leadership development. Then, there comes a time when the leader must selflessly let go of followers who have become good leaders. It would be easier to keep them around, sit back after years of training followers and carrying the burdens of leadership, and delegate to them while enjoying a deserved rest. This is the time when a spiritual leader in the depths of his or her soul and spirit needs to give these followers-leaders to others and their needs, and then laboriously start afresh with the training of others. As a spiritual leader you will be grateful for the followers you have had, pray for them, pleading with love for their success, but you must also let them go. There is true beauty in selfless leadership. As a great leader you must step aside, keep your followers growth alive in your heart, celebrate their departure, and begin again. Working with followers is one of the most difficult aspects of leadership. It is also one of the most rewarding, as the good you have created lives on, extends itself, and enriches many people with its benefits. In the process, this selfless giving to others will enrich your own leadership and life.

STEP TEN

ACCEPT TEN PERSONAL REFLECTIONS

In this last chapter I want to share with you ten practices I have found helpful. I think it would be appropriate to describe myself as an inner leader. When Gilbert Fairholm uses this term he is not referring to a leader with inner spiritual values, although he would want that, and so would I. Rather, he means someone who is in the middle of an organization's structure and has responsibilities to those above and below him or her in the structure and can have positive influence in both directions. I have run a small business, worked in middle management, led a section of an international training movement, been a private consultant, run a conference center, been a university professor and a dean. I have worked in eleven countries for at least several months and in some cases for years. I have had opportunities to present courses, workshops, and conferences on leadership to top administrators in business, healthcare, non-profits, and religion. I have taught courses on leadership at the masters and doctoral levels in several universities. I have observed, reflected, evaluated, and learned from my experiences, and it is from these diverse experiences that I share with you ten reflections that sum up practices I have found helpful. I hope they might help you too.

1. Affirm people.

One of the most important practices I have made my own is to constantly affirm people. I am convinced that everyone in the organization has something very special to contribute, and if I cannot see it, it is my fault. Of course there are always exceptions, and while some may be gifted, they may not be suited to the present organization, and their gifts better used elsewhere. Then a leader's responsibility is to help that person find the best place to work, even if it is elsewhere. It is hard to work with someone whom you think needs to leave, but this too can be an affirming experience when it is clear you are seeking what is best for him or her. However, most people can contribute to the present organization, and it is a leader's task to discover and affirm workers' contributions. In committee meetings I would directly invite everyone to share their opinion on the topic under discussion, calling on them by name and then commenting positively on their contribution, or even disagreeing with them with respect and appreciation. People I have worked with knew that I would call on everyone, and it led to people being better prepared for meetings. At the end of a meeting I used to summarize the work of the group, clearly including the suggestions of everyone—even by name. If the work we did in groups or committees led to a final report I would always let people see themselves in the report. I would use their exact words or the specific ideas they presented, so that they could see they were included. This might lead to a rather clumsy report, but once people had seen themselves affirmed, it could always be edited later, while preserving their basic insights.

When co-workers contribute to the group's common vision the leader becomes an executive to others' ideas. It is important that workers know that their contributions will be treated seriously. Part of affirming them is for the leader to show that what they suggested was implemented. On occasions I have deliberately absented myself from a meeting at the last minute, delegating someone else to run the meeting, and then implementing the group's recommendations even when I was not a part to the discussion. Thus, the group would know their ideas were important. This is a clear indication of the leader being executive to others' ideas.

I have always found it important to keep myself informed about others' achievements. Many co-workers have written reports or articles, and I would read their work and quote them where appropriate, giving them the chance of visibility and open appreciation for their insights. I often wrote to them to compliment them on their work. I would prepare for meetings so as to have something to say about someone's recent successes, so that the whole group could participate in the success of its members. While it is always important never to break confidences, some people do keep their achievements to themselves, and it is good for the whole group to celebrate.

I have always felt a responsibility to affirm those who work with me and those who work for me; however, it is equally necessary to affirm those who are above one in the organization. Leaders need affirming too, and it is supportive to single out their achievements and publicize them as well.

2. Build good social interactions.

I have always kept at my fingertips the psychological stages of a group's development. There are several different ways of thinking about this, and most are good. In each case it is clear that there is no significant development of group growth that does not include a stage in the development of human relationships. There is no possibility of moving to a shared vision or to mature common shared values without this interpersonal stage. Nowadays, we have so many e-mails and so little communication; so many meetings and so little sense of community. I have found that giving adequate attention to the social development of a group will pay high dividends. My wife and I have spent a lot of our own money on socials, dinners, and get togethers for groups we have worked with, finding that when people develop friendship they work together with greater common spirit and mutual appreciation. Groups can be delicate to work with; sometimes members will move in and out of a group, depending on their commitment or what they think they are getting out of it; then the group will draw people in and deliberately push them out, depending on their commitment to the common life of the group. So, the social development is crucial to stability and growth. In any social gatherings a leader must work the crowd, try to meet everyone, make sure people who might be potential opponents meet each other and enjoy each other's company, and introduce people who do not know each other. I have found that socials are hard work, but they can produce good results. Too many administrators are passive at socials, remaining with their in-group, giving the impression they are the focus of attention and not everyone else.

Another way I have found helps good social interaction is the simple practice of trying to answer questions people raise on the same day they ask them, rather than putting it off until they do not know whether you are still working on it or have forgotten it. I generally told people I would have an answer by four o'clock that afternoon or the following afternoon, whichever was appropriate. Then at four o'clock I would phone with an update to say that I had the answer or I did not, and then tell them what had been achieved and when I would have the complete answer. Co-workers appreciated that their questions were significant enough to merit attention and resolution.

In dealing with people from other countries, I have found that it is important to make it clear that I am aware of their culture and even language. I have worked with international organizations where the members spoke different languages and found that even a little effort to speak other languages lets people know how much you appreciate them. If colleagues came from other countries and we would be working together for some time, I would study about their country. This too I have found helps build social and interpersonal relationships.

3. Always do more than you ask of anyone else.

I have always considered this practice to be very important, and when done, to produce excellent results. If you want to be a leader at any level in an organization then you must work hard, in fact, very hard. Whatever your job, you must reach beyond it. Professional commitment—what you do to be professionally successful—is not enough. You must focus on discretionary commitment—that depth of commitment that goes beyond what is required to be a good professional. Many people give the former, few the latter, but it is only the latter that produces great leadership. When individuals or groups come to a meeting you must have already done most of the work. I have been to so many meetings where the chair is totally unprepared. Personally I would prefer to cancel a meeting rather than have one for which I was not completely prepared. This means doing the homework, meeting people beforehand so that there are no surprises, identifying the desired outcomes, making sure critical individuals are well prepared with what you need from them. I always felt I wanted to work hard; I did not want anyone in the group to be working harder than me. Then I knew that when I asked someone to be generous beyond what they planned, they would be less likely to refuse when they had seen how hard I was willing to work.

As part of this approach to work and responsibility, I tried never to evaluate others on what I did not do. I appreciate that sometimes it is possible to know what others should do without doing precisely what they do; then evaluation is possible by you as an outsider. However, as a general rule I dislike evaluating on issues I have not personally done. I find too many administrators expect and demand of others what they themselves are either incapable of doing, or if capable, too lazy or unprofessional to do. I have found that when I need to be involved in evaluating others that a good point of departure is to set up a serious evaluation of myself by others, according to their criteria and methods. I let them do the evaluation professionally and present a report to my supervisor. Then when they see I am willing to be thus involved, they move with more ease into their own evaluation. If my self-evaluation is thorough, then theirs can be also.

So, I would always work harder than I would ask of others, while prudently making sure I was not sucked in to a workaholic approach or potential burnout. Leaders must be aware of the fatigue of dedication. Maintaining balance in one's life is also part of a leader's task. Doing more and being more must go together.

4. Reflect and pray.

I have seen many leaders move from one project to another, doing a lot and achieving little; their cluttered lives reflected in their cluttered approach to administration. I have also seen many leaders incapable of delegating, either because they do not trust anyone to do the job in the way they want, or because they are just simply insecure. So, they accumulate work that their staff should do, and their days are filled with secondary issues that should never be done by someone on their salary scale. Leaders today must be men and women of reflection—what I have called contemplative leaders. Reflection is necessary to maintain the peace of mind needed to make good decisions, to discern between alternative goals and means, to lead in light of values, and to keep one's leadership in line with one's destiny. The higher a leader is in a structure the more he or she must give time to thinking, reflecting, integrating, discerning, and visioning. I always like to begin a day with a period of reflective prayer. I do not see this as a time to plan or to prioritize the issues of the day, but to empty one's mind and heart and to open oneself to the transcendent. If leadership is what God is doing in us, then we must create opportunity for the transformation that comes from beyond us. I am keen on the idea of being here while also being elsewhere. This awareness of living on two horizons of life at the same time means living with a profound sense of presence to the values of this world and to the values of an horizon of life beyond this one that gives meaning to this one.

I find a daily period of reflective prayer helps to cleanse one's mind of problems, possible anger at difficulties that have arisen, resentment at co-workers who have treated us unfairly, and any unworthy attitudes that at times we develop. Then, one can fill one's mind and heart with values that one wants to guide the day. It is a time to give oneself to the call of God, to offer oneself in service of others, to accept the day ahead with its joys and hardships, and to unite oneself in faith, hope, and love to the God of one's vocation to leadership. Prayer is a time to prepare oneself for the day ahead, to start with the right perspective, to empty oneself of false values, and to fill oneself with the values and vision that guide the life of a spiritual leader.

While a period of morning reflection can set the tone for the day, I have always found it important to train myself to live in the presence of God. This training takes effort but there comes a time when it becomes impossible not to live with this awareness, and then it influences one's whole approach to leadership. I do not know when that happened for me, but it did, and I now feel I can live with a constant awareness of how transcendent values must affect all that I do.

5. Live simply as a leader.

Most organizations I have worked for have too many administrators, many of whom have titles and budgets they do not need nor merit. They are competitive with each other internal to the structure, seeking to enlarge their staffs, their budgets, their personal perks. There is so much useless assigning of money, as sections of an organization live beyond their means, unable to give up their slush funds and constant visits to the candy store. They know that the squeaky wheels get the support even when they do not deserve it or need it. In recent years, we have seen what the greed of individuals and organizations can do to a nation, and it has shocked us. But on a lesser scale I have seen similar tendencies in organizations of various kinds all over the world. I believe it is important to live simply as a leader. I have always tried to run a tight budget, never to expect others to subsidize my unit. I do not spend on myself, my office, or my personal budget beyond necessities, and I have worked to create income for others' use. If I could develop a new program that would cover the cost of one person's salary I was happy. I do not believe I have ever asked for what I would not approve for someone else. Moreover, I do not give false expectations to co-workers regarding salaries or organizational change. Big is not better, more is not an improvement, and personal self-aggrandizement is of no significant value.

A spiritual leader can give an example of what good leadership is all about. A leader should oversee significant development wherever possible. Some of the organizations I have administered have grown a lot in my time of leadership. However, it is important that the growth be genuine, within the parameters of good budgeting, and without empty showiness and artificial growth. Lots of things can be done in an organization and they cost nothing, whereas many other things cost a lot and accomplish very little. Some administrators have an insatiable need of money, personnel, office space, and the perks of the elite. Some of this can be done without harming anyone, but often it is at others' expense. A spiritual leader must work for justice, fairness, and take care of others, rather than feathering his or her own nest.

Living simply means having responsibility for the whole organization in which you administer a unit. I have worked in several countries where the organizations never became a community but co-existed as independent units within a federation, each competing with others for available resources. A spiritual leader shows responsibility for the entire community in which he or she works, showing interest in the growth and development of the whole. Living simply as a leader is, to me, a prophetic witness and one of the most neglected aspects of spiritual leadership and also one of the most difficult.

6. Choose to work with opposition.

Every organization has some members who are always critical, challenging almost everything that a leader tries to do. They seem to feel they have a responsibility to criticize everything. These professional irritants never seem to change or go away, but provide an alternative picture of almost every issue. However, these irritants often represent the views of many within the organization and generally have a significant and faithful following. I do not think I have ever had a significant argument with any such individuals, I value their role in the organization, and appreciate that they have gifts to contribute. I would not call these people prophetical in their denunciations, but rather organizational irritants whose voices need to be heard. I have had to work with many committees and groups in various countries and have found that sometimes these people are elected by their peers to provide an alternative position to administrators who like to stack the committees in their own favor. This is fine and when thrown together with these people I have always worked with them, valuing their contribution. However, I would go further, and deliberately choose these individuals when setting up groups within the organization for discussion of important issues. Moreover, I never brought them in to tame them or persuade them to my views. Rather, I brought them in to learn from them, to give the committee wider acceptance, and to enrich the conclusions of the group. I have always found these people to be very good, to have the best interests of the organization at heart, and to contribute generously. Moreover, the larger community was always more likely to accept the result of the group's work when such professional irritants were a part of the process. When at the end of debate some still felt opposed to the general view, I would always include a minority report to give respect and visibility to their views.

When dealing with group discussion with oppositional figures as part of the debate, the group's discussion will need some direction and gentle guidance, so that it does not get out of hand or become polarizing. But that is not difficult to do when you presume the good will of all and act accordingly. There have been times when I had to spend some private time with the oppositional figures, appeal to their good will for the success of the group's work, and urge them to use more patience and understanding of others. I never found such appeals rejected, but rather supported. Certainly, most organizations I have worked with have had administrators who stacked committees with their supporters, and so outcomes were predetermined. On such occasions little dynamic growth takes place, no synergy, just the same old ideas repeated over and over again. An organization's professional irritants can bring liveliness to the discussion and new life to the direction of the organization. Moreover, they often stimulate the regular rank and file to think differently.

7. Be a free voice.

In my earlier life I had the opportunity to learn firsthand from one of the most prophetical people of this age. He insisted that the thing he valued most was to be a free voice, not controlled by the organization's elite. I have treasured this quality all my life; to speak my mind freely, to say what I think needs to be said, to be indebted to no one. I must acknowledge that I have been very fortunate in the supervisors for whom I have worked; they have given me the freedom that is needed to be outspoken without fear of reprisals. I have been fortunate while others have been trapped in the insecure controls of unbalanced leaders. Being outspoken requires trust, respect for those who give you the freedom to speak, and a readiness to listen to others who choose to be outspoken. I will not do anything I disapprove of; if I see something I consider unjust I want to challenge it; if something is contrary to the mission and values of the organization I will insist on saying so. I try to speak firmly and respectfully.

There are some things that must be said. At times, I feel the need to challenge something I see to be wrong, even though I know that people who hear will do nothing about it. They will hide from the problem or find excuses, but I will not give them the luxury of ignorance—"I didn't know that!" I want to make people face up to the issues. However, one must be clear about the issues and what one wants to achieve. It is no use fighting to win and then wonder what it is you won.

I have often chosen to write to the top administrators in organizations to point out what I consider unfair, unjust, or unethical practices. Addressing one's correspondence to the vice president for ethical and social responsibility, when you are aware that probably no such position exists, can still point out that the organization should be concerned about these things. Top administrators get away with far too much today, and they need to be made accountable. So, I often reach out beyond my own organization to challenge leaders in other organizations to fulfill their moral, ethical, and leadership responsibilities.

If you want to be a free voice within an organization then you must take care to avoid arrogance and self-righteousness. I have mentioned the importance of humility for a leader, and that need is highlighted again on this current issue. In situations like this it is useful to have a mentor, close friend, or spouse, who will help keep you focused, honest, and fair in your assessment of others.

8. Plan from hope.

I have often been involved in organizational planning, establishing goals and objectives, facilitating a strategic plan, a marketing plan, and outcomes assessment. All these are helpful. At the same time planning often prolongs the best of the present into the future, even though the best of the present is often not worth keeping. Personally I have always planned from the future to the present and not from the present to the future. This kind of prospective planning is hope-filled and an exercise in establishing a Christian vision. I find that in planning, too many people get bogged down in the present's problems and restrictions, quickly pointing out that "such and such has been tried," "we have tried that and it doesn't work," "we don't have the resources," and so on. The approach to planning that I have used both in my personal life and in organizations I have worked with is to plan backwards from an ideal future. First, I would ask people to have a good look at the present since we cannot ignore it; identify problems, potentialities for good, obstacles to future growth. Then we evaluate carefully how we see ourselves as an organization—what are our strengths and weaknesses. Second, it is important to lay aside the present and to create an ideal future, for say the next five years, making sure it is really something people find attractive, worth working for, that will meet their hopes and dreams. Third, with those who work with me in the organization I would take the ideal future and confront it with the present, identifying areas that need change to reach the ideal future. Fourth, we would concretize the ideal future in attainable goals for five years from now, trying to establish confidence that we can reach those goals. Fifth, I plan backwards from the presumed attained goals of five years hence; if we are to get there in five years where must we be in three years, in two years, in one year, and so on. Sixth, we would decide who would be responsible for each goal, what resources would be made available, who would do what, how, and why.

I have rarely found a group who did not meet the goals it set for itself. In fact, often a group would get ahead of itself and then have to reset more challenging goals. This approach fills the participants with hope and satisfaction. It energizes participants and stimulates a common sense of achievement. Hope is the great motivator of people in organizations, and without hope decay is inevitable. This process includes prayer and discernment more than planning techniques. When people look to the future with hope they do not get bogged down in the problems of the present. This form of planning must be carefully monitored, and I have found that it is important to keep everyone on schedule, evaluating progress regularly.

9. Keep working life in perspective.

I have mentioned the importance of discretionary commitment—doing more than is professionally required, and I have insisted that I have always tried to do more than I would ask of anyone else. However, this must be kept within the context of regular working life. Work influences life, but it is not the whole of life. I have seen lots of workaholics whose endless work hides their escape from relationships and real life situations. I have seen groups of people each of whom is afraid to be the first to go home in the evening, lest one be viewed as less dedicated than those who remain, even though no one is really doing anything significant. Nowadays, some have an almost addictive approach to computer work beyond the regular office hours or contractual commitments, and they need to re-learn how to live for real in an unreal or virtual world. How often have we all seen workers absorbed on the computer, or iPod, or cell phone, while sitting in a restaurant opposite their spouse and never communicating a word. Work has a purpose, a context, and its own limitations. For many it takes control of life and that is unhealthy, and it defeats the purpose of work.

I have always worked hard, but I have always—with very rare exceptions—gone home on time, I have not continued my work at home, I never worked on weekends or vacations. My wife and I had the practice of discussing work on the way home, but once in the house it was finished until we returned to work the next day. Jobs are generally tailored for a working day and a working week. Nowadays, workers can often choose times to work, work from home, or even work on projects without specific office hours. All this is good but I have found it must be controlled, so that work does not absorb life, for then problems arise that can have destructive influences on one's leadership and life.

Part of avoiding overtime for me is that I wanted to retire from my job at the right time. Too many leaders stay on the job too long, as if they were indispensable, which they never are. I wanted to retire when there were still some around me who would have liked me to stay. I have seen too many leaders whose workers long for them to go, and they stay on, losing respect from all around them. No one is indispensable, and when you leave people will forget you in a matter of a couple of weeks. There are always those leaders who have unfortunately identified themselves with their working life and so do not know what to do with themselves in retirement. It is important that a leader have a balanced life, with many interests, so that when he or she chooses to retire the leader can move into a fulfilling retirement. Work continues in retirement even though one's job or career ends. Those who were addicted or unbalanced in their approach to working life will carry those false values into retirement and become competitive in retirement as they were in their working lives.

10. Create new projects.

This is an unusual suggestion, and I admit it cannot always be done. Much depends on the kind of work you are involved in. I have always been involved in work that allowed for new projects and the excitement and creativity that accompany such endeavors. I have not been involved in developing new projects just simply to expand, but I do believe that they help maintain vitality, give opportunities for implementing the vision in new ways, and can challenge all to stretch the mission of the organization. Moreover, we live in times of job insecurity, when budget demands often mean cutbacks that can affect the very dedicated in an organization. I have found that keeping an eye on the possibility of new projects helps maintain the vision of where you want to go with the organization and also how you can preserve people's jobs. New projects also help focus co-workers' attention on what is essential to the common vision, and even if a project does not materialize, the thinking and planning that accompany the preliminaries to new projects keep people revising the values they hold and how they can continue to implement them. Creating new projects brings excitement, creativity, common commitment, and a future outlook. Sometimes, you find that thinking about a new project brings renewed life to current components of the organization's work.

Every year, I would spend time planning to see if there was some way I could develop an aspect of the organization. It might be expanding to another city or to another country. When working in leadership training, I rented planes and sent instructors to three of four different cities at a time, dropping off one here and one there on the way to a final point of contact. I had over twenty-five different cities involved in the project. Computers have made distant learning projects easy to develop, although maintaining quality is now the key challenge, and it is better to omit the developments than do them poorly. New projects, even volunteer ones, help attract others to share in the common mission and expand the effectiveness of the organization.

Keeping a portion of your time for project planning keeps you thinking about essentials. It is a way of evaluating your current endeavors and whether they can be modified to achieve your new goals. I find the creativity needed helps focus on hope, allows the organization to constantly adapt, keeps workers alive to change, and brings in new income as old projects die.

I have personally found the call to leadership an integral part of my life and purpose. Growth has taken place in the variety of situations and institutions that have been part of my work experience. But I am profoundly grateful that I have never equated the job with life, rather, I have embraced work as a creative and fulfilling part of it. I would challenge leaders who want to grow and to integrate their work, leadership, and life to constantly remind themselves to keep all in perspective. Being a spiritual leader is not easy; it takes time and dedication. May some of the suggestions in this book help those who strive to serve others through their leadership.

Readers interested in spiritual leadership can read my blog and contribute a comment or become a guest blogger

leonarddoohan.wordpress.com

Once a month I contribute a guest presentation for the internationally recognized blog on leadership linked2leadership.com

See Leonard Doohan's webpage at *leonarddoohan.com*

THREE BOOKS ON SPIRITUAL LEADERSHIP

How to Become a Great Spiritual Leader: Ten Steps and a Hundred Suggestions

This is a book for daily meditation. It has a single focus—how to become a great spiritual leader. It is a book on the spirituality of a leader's personal life. It presumes that leadership is a vocation, and that it results from an inner transformation. The book proposes ten steps that individuals can take to enable this process of transformation, and a hundred suggestions to make this transformation real and lasting. It is a unique book in the literature on leadership.

This book is the third in a series on leadership. The first, *Spiritual Leadership: The Quest for Integrity* gave the foundations of leadership today. The second, *Courageous Hope: The Call of Leadership*, gave the contemporary characteristics and qualities of leadership. This third book focuses on the spirituality of the leader.

Courageous Hope: The Call of Leadership

This book's focus on leadership and hope is very appropriate given today's climate of distrust that many find results in a sense of hopelessness in their current leaders. Individuals and organizations are desperate for leaders of hope. Many books on leadership point to the need for inner motivation, but that inner motivation must be hope in new possibilities for a changed future. It is hope that gives a meaningful expression to leadership and enables the leader to be creative in dealing with the present. More than anything else it is a vision of hope that can excite and empower leaders to inspire others to strive for a common vision.

"Doohan strengthens our resolve. He restores our hope. And in an echo of Robert Frost, he is not only a teacher, but an awakener. May this book find you in a place where your will to grow is matched by an inner radiance to serve and help heal those around you... the reading will meet you there and the end result will be a gift to the world." **Shann Ray Ferch, PhD, MFA** Professor and Chair, Doctoral Program in Leadership Studies, Gonzaga University. Editor, International Journal of Servant Leadership.

"Read every word of this book. Leaders stuck in the past, afraid to face the future, afraid to take a risk because they might be wrong need an infusion of *Courageous Hope*. People are not looking for a simple, blind-faith hope. They are looking for leaders with a deeper understanding of hope as described in this book. **Mary McFarland, PhD** Professor, and Former Dean of undergraduate through doctoral programs in Leadership. International consultant in leadership and education.

"Ask people who were alive during the Great Depression what a huge difference Franklin Roosevelt made in their lives by giving them reasons to be hopeful. Ask people who were alive during the papacy of John XXIII what they loved most about him, and chances are they'll say that "good Pope John" gave them hope for the future. Read *Courageous Hope* and learn how to be that kind of leader yourself." **Mitch Finley,** Author of over 30 award winning books.

Spiritual Leadership: The Quest for Integrity

In eight clear and challenging chapters, the reader is invited to partake of a rich menu of reflections on the meaning of spiritual leadership and how it can transform one's role in the workplace, ensuring a collaborative environment of trust and confidence that energizes not only the culture of an organization, but also the effective accomplishment of its mission.

Leonard Doohan's highly readable book presents leadership as a call motivated by faith and love that results in a change of life, a conversion, and a breakthrough to a new vision of one's role in the world.

"Leonard Doohan's *Spiritual Leadership* is a profound and caring work . . . I highly recommend it to anyone interested in the spiritual meaning of servant leadership." **Larry C. Spears.**

"'The leader within,' . . . is well served by Leonard Doohan's book, *Spiritual Leadership*. It is a profound guidebook for leaders of the future, who live their values, who keep the faith. **Frances Hesselbein.** Chair, Leader to Leader Institute

Dr. Leonard Doohan's new volume on *Spiritual Leadership* reaches beyond, or perhaps better, beneath the many current volumes on leadership which emphasize skill sets, techniques, and learned habits." **Robert J. Spitzer, SJ, PhD.** President and CEO, Magis Institute

Another book of interest

Enjoying Retirement: Living Life to the Fullest

A book for leaders in retirement. This book is for a new kind of retiree—including the baby-boomer generation—who seeks to deal with retirement years not as an end of usefulness but as a major period in life with its own challenges that need practical responses and depth of understanding. Christian spirituality refers to the way we live our daily lives in the challenge of faith. Clearly, the years of retirement offer the most important occasion for each of us to respond to this challenge of making a new beginning.

This wise and engaging book offers wonderful opportunities to discover how to approach retirement—now as much as a third of life for many—with enthusiasm, anticipation, creativity, and enjoyment as the best and blessed time of our lives.

These last three books are available from paulistpress.com and all are available from amazon.com

Made in the USA
San Bernardino, CA
18 May 2015